LITERATURE GUIDE

GCSE

Pride and Prejudice

First published 2003
exclusively for WHSmith by
Hodder & Stoughton Educational
338 Euston Road
London
NW1 3BH

ISBN 0 340 87295 0

Copyright © 2003 Michael Kerrigan
Introduction ('How to study') copyright © 2003 Tony Buzan

All rights reserved. No part of this publication may be reproduced or transmitted in any form or by any means, electronic or mechanical, including photocopying, recording or any information storage and retrieval system, without permission in writing from the publisher or under licence from the Copyright Licensing Agency Limited. Further details of such licences (for reprographic reproduction) may be obtained from the Copyright Licensing Agency Limited, of 90 Tottenham Court Road, London W1P 9HE

Illustrations: Karen Donnelly
Mind Maps ®: Anne Jones

Typeset by Transet Limited, Leamington Spa, England.
Printed in Great Britain for Hodder & Stoughton Educational, a division of Hodder Headline Plc, 338 Euston Road, London NW1 3BH by Cox & Wyman Ltd., Reading, Berkshire.

CONTENTS

How to study	v
How to use this guide	ix
•Key to icons	x
Background	1
The story of *Pride and Prejudice*	6
Who's who?	**12**
• Elizabeth	12
• Darcy	13
• Jane	13
• Mr Bennet	14
• Mrs Bennet	14
• Lydia	15
• Mary	15
• Kitty	15
• Bingley	16
• Wickham	16
• Charlotte	17
• Mrs Gardiner	17
• Mr Collins	17
• Lady Catherine	18
Themes	**20**
• Family	20
• Marriage	21
• Gentility	22
• Accomplishments	23
• Reading	24
• Growth	26
Commentary	**29**

iii

Topics for discussion and brainstorming	**75**
How to get an 'A' in English Literature	**77**
The exam essay	**78**
Model answer and essay plan	**79**
Glossary of literary terms	**83**
Index	**85**

How to Study

There are five important things you must know about your brain and memory to revolutionise the way you study:

- ◆ how your memory ('recall') works *while* you are learning
- ◆ how your memory works *after* you have finished learning
- ◆ how to use Mind Maps – a special technique for helping you with all aspects of your studies
- ◆ how to increase your reading speed
- ◆ how to prepare for tests and exams.

Recall during learning
– THE NEED FOR BREAKS

When you are studying, your memory can concentrate, understand and remember well for between 20 and 45 minutes at a time. Then it needs a break. If you carry on for longer than this without a break your memory starts to break down. If you study for hours non-stop, you will remember only a small fraction of what you have been trying to learn, and you will have wasted hours of valuable time.

So, ideally, *study for less than an hour*, then take a five to ten minute break. During the break listen to music, go for a walk, do some exercise, or just daydream. (Daydreaming is a necessary brain-power booster – geniuses do it regularly.) During the break your brain will be sorting out what it has been learning, and you will go back to your books with the new information safely stored and organised in your memory banks. We recommend breaks at regular intervals as you work through the Literature Guides. Make sure you take them!

Recall after learning
– THE WAVES OF YOUR MEMORY

What do you think begins to happen to your memory straight after you have finished learning something? Does it immediately start forgetting? No! Your brain actually *increases* its power and carries on remembering. For a short time after your study session, your brain integrates the information, making a more complete picture of everything it has just learnt. Only then does the rapid decline in memory begin, and as much as 80 per cent of what you have learnt can be forgotten in a day.

However, if you catch the top of the wave of your memory, and briefly review (look back over) what you have been studying at the correct time, the memory is stamped in far more strongly, and stays at the crest of the wave for a much longer time. To maximise your brain's power to remember, take a few minutes and use a Mind Map to review what you have learnt at the end of a day. Then review it at the end of a week, again at the end of a month, and finally a week before your test or exam. That way you'll ride your memory wave all the way there – and beyond!

The Mind Map®
– A PICTURE OF THE WAY YOU THINK

Do you like taking notes? More importantly, do you like having to go back over and learn them before tests or exams? Most students I know certainly do not! And how do you take your notes? Most people take notes on lined paper, using blue or black ink. The result, visually, is boring! And what does *your* brain do when it is bored? It turns off, tunes out, and goes to sleep! Add a dash of colour, rhythm, imagination, and the whole note-taking process becomes much more fun, uses more of your brain's abilities, and improves your recall and understanding.

A Mind Map mirrors the way your brain works. It can be used for note-taking from books or in class, for reviewing what you have just studied, and for essay planning for coursework and in tests or exams. It uses all your memory's natural techniques to build up your rapidly growing 'memory muscle'.

HOW TO STUDY

You will find Mind Maps throughout this book. Study them, add some colour, personalise them, and then have a go at drawing your own – you'll remember them far better! Stick them in your files and on your walls for a quick-and-easy review of the topic.

HOW TO DRAW A MIND MAP

1 Start in the middle of the page. This gives your brain the maximum room for its thoughts.
2 Always start by drawing a small picture or symbol. Why? Because a picture is worth a thousand words to your brain. And try to use at least three colours, as colour helps your memory even more.
3 Let your thoughts flow, and write or draw your ideas on coloured branching lines connected to your central image. These key symbols and words are the headings for your topic. Start like the Mind Map on page 12.
4 Then add facts and ideas by drawing more, smaller, branches on to the appropriate main branches, just like a tree.
5 Always print your word clearly on its line. Use only one word per line.
6 To link ideas and thoughts on different branches, use arrows, colours, underlining, and boxes (see page 19).

HOW TO READ A MIND MAP

1 Begin in the centre, the focus of your topic.
2 The words/images attached to the centre are like chapter headings, read them next.
3 Always read out from the centre, in every direction (even on the left-hand side, where you will have to read from right to left, instead of the usual left to right).

USING MIND MAPS

Mind Maps are a versatile tool – use them for taking notes in class or from books, for solving problems, for brainstorming with friends, and for reviewing and working for tests or exams – their uses are endless! You will find them invaluable for planning essays for coursework and exams. Number your main branches in the order in which you want to use them and off you go – the main headings for your essay are done and all your ideas are logically organised!

Super speed reading

It seems incredible, but it's been proved – the faster you read, the more you understand and remember! So here are some tips to help you to practise reading faster – you'll cover the ground more quickly, remember more, and have more time left for both work and play.

◆ First read the whole text (whether it's a lengthy book or an exam or test paper) very quickly, to give your brain an overall idea of what's ahead and get it working. (It's like sending out a scout to look at the territory you have to cover – it's much easier when you know what to expect!) Then read the text again for more detailed information.
◆ Have the text a reasonable distance away from your eyes. In this way your eye/brain system will be able to see more at a glance, and will naturally begin to read faster.
◆ Take in groups of words at a time. Rather than reading 'slowly and carefully' read faster, more enthusiastically.
◆ Take in phrases rather than single words while you read.
◆ Use a guide. Your eyes are designed to follow movement, so a thin pencil underneath the lines you are reading, moved smoothly along, will 'pull' your eyes to faster speeds.

Preparing for tests and exams

◆ Review your work systematically. Cram at the start of your course, not the end, and avoid 'exam panic'!
◆ Use Mind Maps throughout your course, and build a Master Mind Map for each subject – a giant Mind Map that summarises everything you know about the subject.
◆ Use memory techniques such as mnemonics (verses or systems for remembering things like dates and events).
◆ Get together with one or two friends to study, compare Mind Maps, and discuss topics.

AND FINALLY...

Have *fun* while you learn – it has been shown that students who make their studies enjoyable understand and remember everything better and get the highest grades. I wish you and your brain every success!

(Tony Buzan)

HOW TO USE THIS GUIDE

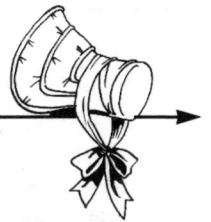

This guide assumes that you have already read *Pride and Prejudice*, although you could read 'Background' and 'The Story of *Pride and Prejudice*' before that. It is best to use the guide alongside the play. You could read the 'Who's Who?' and 'Themes' sections without referring to the novel, but you will get more out of these sections if you do refer to it to check the points made in these sections, and especially when thinking about the questions designed to test your recall and help you think about the novel.

The 'Commentary' section can be used in a number of ways. One way is to read a chapter in the novel, and then read the commentary for that section. Keep on until you come to a test section, test yourself – and then have a break! Alternatively, read the Commentary for a chapter, then read that section in the novel, then go back to the Commentary. Find out what works best for you.

'Topics for discussion and brainstorming' gives topics that could well feature in exams or provide the basis for coursework. It would be particularly useful for you to discuss them with friends, or brainstorm them using Mind Map techniques (see p. vi).

'How to get an "A" in English Literature' gives valuable advice on what to look for in a text, and what skills you need to develop in order to achieve your personal best.

'The exam essay' is a useful 'night before' reminder of how to tackle exam questions, though of course it's better to look at it well in advance. 'Model answer and essay plan' gives an example of an A-grade essay and the Mind Map and plan used to write it.

THE QUESTIONS

Whenever you come across a question in the guide with a star ✪ in front of it, think about it for a moment. You could even jot down a few words in rough to focus your mind. There is not usually a 'right' answer to these questions: it is important for you to develop your own opinions if you want to get an 'A'. The 'Test yourself' sections are designed to take you about 10–20 minutes each – which will be time well spent. Take a short break after each one.

Page numbers

Chapter and page references are to the Penguin Classics edition, edited by Tony Tanner. If you have another edition, the page numbers may be slightly different, although the chapter numbers will be the same.

Key to icons

THEMES

A **theme** is an idea explored by an author. Whenever a theme is dealt with in the guide, the appropriate icon is used. This means you can find where a theme is mentioned just by flicking through the book. Go on – try it now!

Family

Accomplishment

Marriage

Reading

Gentility

Growth

STYLE AND LANGUAGE

This icon is used in the Commentary wherever there is a special section on the author's choice of words and **imagery** (a kind of word picture used to make an idea come alive).

 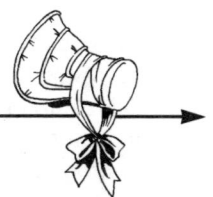

Pride and Prejudice started life under a different title altogether. As *First Impressions*, the story of Elizabeth and Darcy was sent to a London publisher in 1796–7 – and rejected. That decision seems incredible to us now. Just how shortsighted the publisher was really being, though, we cannot know, as the text of this novel has been lost.

A *romantic romance?*

It must have been a strange time to be the editor in a publishing house, since readers' tastes were in the midst of one of the most profound shifts they have ever undergone: from the 'Classicism' of the eighteenth century to the 'Romanticism' of the nineteenth. A public which had prized the sort of symmetrical construction associated with Greek and Roman architecture, and the elegant expression and detached, ironic wit associated with the classical poets, was starting to find such things repellently cold and clinical. Poets like Wordsworth, Keats and Shelley were promoting a new spontaneity of expression, a new extravagance of emotion and, in the enormously popular writings of Byron, readers were learning to love a new breed of brooding, masterful heroes.

Born in 1764, Jane Austen was by education and upbringing a product of the 'classical' eighteenth century – especially because she was brought up not in trend-setting London but in the provinces, where new ideas were slow to catch on. She was suspicious of Romanticism's emotional extremism, and scathing – often hilariously so – about its practitioners' tendency to take themselves too seriously.

Despite her scepticism, Jane Austen could not help being influenced by the new movement, and its influence can be detected in *Pride and Prejudice* – not just in its strong, silent hero but more generally in the spirit that gives such emotional depth to what might easily have been no more than a clever-clever comedy. That is all Jane Austen's first known novel seems to us today. *Lady Susan* was written a year before *First Impressions* in 1795, and is very much a work of the eighteenth century: slick, smart and to our way of thinking a bit heartless. Perhaps *First Impressions* itself would have been no more to our taste. In the event, well over a decade would pass before the extensively revised *Pride and Prejudice* was sent off to a publisher – this time successfully. It came out in 1813, by which time a new century had begun and a new attitude to writing and feeling had come into play – one much more like our own.

A *working class?*

Yet the world of *Pride and Prejudice* still seems strange to us. For one thing, nobody seems to do any work. Like Jane Austen's other novels, *Pride and Prejudice* is set among the English gentry, a class whose wealth is passed on from one generation to the next. The men and women who actually work the land that provides this wealth, who build the houses, drive the carriages and serve the suppers of the gentry, are all but invisible in Jane Austen's fiction.

This seems strange – not to say objectionable – to the reader today. It is, however, an accurate reflection of how the world would have been seen by the real-life gentry of Jane Austen's time; by Jane Austen herself and her family, come to that. Such people would not have doubted their entitlement to a life of visiting and entertaining, nor the duty of the masses to serve them obediently and unobtrusively.

They did, after all, have their own troubles. Barred by their status from the shame of working for a living, the Bennet girls in *Pride and Prejudice* are in a sense the victims of privilege. For, genteel as they are, they are not rich. The small country house and estate that justifies their father's claim to be a gentleman has been 'entailed' by an ancestor who has decreed (as in a sexist age so many did) that if Mr Bennet has no male heir his property must go to a relation he's never met, Mr Collins, leaving his own daughters with nothing.

BACKGROUND

The marriage market

For the Bennet girls, as for thousands of young ladies like them in real life, not just emotional fulfilment but material survival will depend on their finding a husband. Preferably a husband they can love – but failing that, *any* husband. We should not underestimate Elizabeth's courage in spurning Mr Collins's proposal, grotesque as he seems to us – nor the risk she is taking in turning him down. Her decision, of course, will appear to have been the right one when she finds the man of her dreams in the form of Mr Darcy.

Such storybook endings were not given to all. While admiring and envying Elizabeth's reckless defiance, most of *Pride and Prejudice's* first female readers would have understood Charlotte Lucas's meek acceptance of Collins's proposal – and even considered her lucky to be asked. For the young lady in Jane Austen's day, being left on the shelf was more than a humiliation: it might mean destitution.

So, for all the apparent ease and leisure of the life described in *Pride and Prejudice*, people are certainly working. They are labouring away at visiting, receiving guests, attending balls, making and maintaining the social contacts that will facilitate the making of matrimonial matches. They are practising the piano, working at their embroidery – polishing the 'accomplishments' it is thought will make them attractive to prospective husbands.

When people in Jane Austen's day talked about the 'marriage market', they meant it almost literally. The right match could make a family, the wrong one – or none at all – could ruin it. An unscrupulous young man might marry for money, as Wickham attempts to do with Mary King, or even 'steal an heiress', as he has tried earlier to do with Georgiana Darcy. Similarly, the girl who caught a wealthy husband might transform her family's condition, as Jane and Elizabeth's marriages will transform the condition of the Bennet family.

In such circumstances, love was a luxury, as the realistic streak in *Pride and Prejudice* recognises. But luxuries are prized all the more in times of shortage: to the young girl looking at a future in which some sort of compromise – whether emotional or economic – was practically inevitable, the novel's romantic, escapist element would have spoken even more powerfully than it does to us.

Don't mention the War

You might not think it, but *Pride and Prejudice* is a war novel. Like work, war is something the novel and its characters never really acknowledge, though it is ever-present. Though to Lydia and Kitty the chief purpose of the army is to provide handsome, dashingly uniformed young officers to flirt with, Britain was actually at war with France during the time when the action of *Pride and Prejudice* takes place.

And not just France, England's traditional enemy, but Revolutionary France. In 1789, the French populace had risen up to overthrow their monarchy, and in the terror that followed, not only the King and Queen but some 30,000 more men and women associated with the oppressive old regime had been marched to the guillotine. By the time Jane Austen was writing *First Impressions* in the mid-1790s things were settling down. The spectre of revolutionary violence still loomed large, though, and would have disturbed the English ruling class of which Jane Austen, a country clergyman's daughter, was in her own small way a member.

In fact, English aristocratic anxiety was increasingly justified – because France's new-found stability came at a price. The French government was taking its public's mind off a difficult domestic situation by going to war with neighbouring countries. Thanks largely to the brilliant efforts of one young general, Napoleon Bonaparte, this tactic was rewarded with a string of glorious victories. By 1804, indeed, Napoleon was in a position to crown himself Emperor. In the decade that followed, when Jane Austen would have been working on the revised novel we know as *Pride and Prejudice*, Napoleon's armies were rampaging more or less unhindered across the length and breadth of Europe. Of course, this posed a threat to England itself. If the likelihood of revolution seemed to have diminished, invasion remained a real possibility.

Even so, the continental battlefields would have seemed unthinkably remote to most of the British public. Today quite

BACKGROUND

trivial events are reported instantaneously, worldwide. But news of the French Revolution had taken almost three weeks to reach one Norfolk parish. More than this, though, war was becoming the business of Britain. Building ships, manufacturing weapons and uniforms created employment, and the economy was booming. In addition, while war brought the danger of death or hideous injuries, it also offered a soldier's or sailor's pay to boys from poor families, and a career as an officer to those born higher up the social scale. Jane Austen came from a genteel but by no means wealthy family, and two of her own brothers prospered in the Royal Navy, one rising to the rank of Senior Admiral of the Fleet.

Many readers are surprised that *Pride and Prejudice* does not engage more obviously with this historical context. This merely reflects the reality of the time, however. War in the early years of the nineteenth century was such a constant thing in England that it was taken for granted, and seemed so remote for the majority of those at home that it could be easily ignored.

Yet there remained the real possibility of invasion; there was still an edge of anxiety about the stability of society. The England of Jane Austen was thus poised delicately between perfect prosperity and total disaster. The same sense of precarious happiness can be found in *Pride and Prejudice*. The Bennet girls have been born to an elegant country-house existence yet, thanks to an ancestor's instruction to a lawyer, the death of their father could bring it all crashing down. Elizabeth and Jane will in their marriages find both love and money: for both, however, things could easily have turned out very differently.

now you're familiar with the background, take some time out before moving into the foreground and looking at what actually happens in Pride and Prejudice

THE STORY OF PRIDE AND PREJUDICE

A rich young man has moved into **Netherfield** Hall. Mrs **Bennet** decides he'll be just the husband for one of her daughters. Mr **Bingley** seems a nice young man, and he obviously likes the eldest Bennet girl, **Jane**. His friend **Darcy** isn't so likeable though.

Mr **Collins** arrives for an unexpected visit, hoping to marry one of the Bennet girls. Jane is his first target, but when Mrs Bennet tells him she's all but engaged he settles for **Elizabeth**. She, meanwhile, is much taken with Mr **Wickham**, a handsome, charming officer who's just joined the regiment in Meryton. She is astonished to hear that he was the boyhood friend of Mr **Darcy**, whose schemings have deprived him of his living.

Collins proposes, but Elizabeth turns him down. Mrs Bennet is furious, but Mr Bennet backs his daughter up. Next thing Elizabeth knows, Collins has proposed to her friend **Charlotte** – and been accepted. Meanwhile, **Jane** has been left depressed by the news that Mr **Bingley** has gone to London and probably won't be back.

Mrs Bennet's brother, Mr **Gardiner**, and his wife, come to visit. It's agreed that **Jane** will stay with them in London for a while. On her way to visit **Charlotte** and her new husband in Kent, **Elizabeth** stops off in London to see Jane: her aunt invites her to join herself and Mr Gardiner on a tour to the **Lake** District the following summer. Charlotte seems content in her new home, absurd as her husband is. Darcy arrives to visit his aunt, **Lady Catherine de Bourgh**. Praising Darcy one day, a cousin of his tells Elizabeth how he saved his friend Bingley from a 'most imprudent marriage'. She is angry to think that this marriage would have been with **Jane**.

Darcy proposes to an astonished Elizabeth, who refuses, telling him he has destroyed her sister's happiness, not to mention **Wickham's** prospects. Out walking next day, she is accosted by Darcy, who gives her a letter defending his conduct. Back in Hertfordshire her sisters are hoping Mr Bennet will take the

THE STORY OF PRIDE AND PREJUDICE

family to **Brighton**, where the regiment is to be posted. In the event, **Lydia** is invited down by an officer's wife.

Elizabeth sets off with the **Gardiners**, though for lack of time they'll only be going to **Derbyshire**. Elizabeth is appalled when her aunt suggests a sightseeing visit to **Darcy's** house at **Pemberley**. She is mortified when, walking in the grounds there next day, they meet the owner himself. But he is kind and courteous to Elizabeth and the Gardiners. Next day he brings his party to visit them at the inn: his sister **Georgiana** isn't proud, as she has heard: only shy. **Bingley** is as friendly as ever.

Elizabeth hears that **Lydia** has run away to Scotland with **Wickham**. **Darcy** arrives to find Elizabeth white with shock: she tells him the whole story and he goes off grim-faced. Back at Longbourn, Jane is holding the fort. Mr **Gardiner** persuades Mr Bennet to return home while he hunts for the runaways in London. News comes at last that they have been found and are to be married. The newly-weds visit before heading north to **Wickham's** new posting, Lydia letting slip that **Darcy** was at her wedding. Elizabeth writes to ask Mrs **Gardiner** what he was doing there, only to be told that it was he who had traced the couple and paid **Wickham** off.

Back now at Netherfield, **Bingley's** feelings for Jane seem undiminished, but Elizabeth cannot read **Darcy's** manner. **Bingley** and Jane become engaged. Out of the blue, Lady Catherine comes, demanding that Elizabeth promises not to marry **Darcy**, which she refuses to do. Some days later, **Darcy** visits with Bingley. He asks Elizabeth if she still feels about him as she did when she rejected him before. No, she replies, she feels completely differently.

THE STORY OF PRIDE AND PREJUDICE

connections between events

1 Mr Bingley arrives at Netherfield

2 Nobody likes his friend Mr Darcy

3 Mr Collins comes to visit his cousins

4 But Mr Wickham is much more appealing

5 Collins proposes: Lizzy turns him down

6 He has more luck with Charlotte Lucas

THE STORY OF PRIDE AND PREJUDICE

7 Lizzy visits Charlotte and meets Lady Catherine

8 Darcy proposes: his turn to be turned down

9 Elizabeth goes with Gardiners on Peak District tour

10 Meets Darcy at Pemberley: a new man, it seems

11 Lydia's elopement ruins it all

12 Lydia and Wickham to be married, we hear

13 Lydia lets slip that Darcy was at her wedding

14 Darcy proposes to Elizabeth again – this time she says yes

PRIDE AND PREJUDICE

How much can you remember?

Try filling in the missing words in this alternative version without looking at the original. Feel free to use your own words if they mean the same thing.

A rich young man has moved into _____ Hall. Mrs _____ decides he'll be just the husband for one of her daughters. Mr _____ seems a nice young man, and he obviously likes the eldest Bennet girl, _____. His friend _____ isn't so likeable though.

Mr _____ arrives for an unexpected visit, hoping to marry one of the Bennet girls. Jane is his first target, but when Mrs Bennet tells him she's all but engaged he settles for _____. She, meanwhile, is much taken with Mr _____, a handsome, charming officer who's just joined the regiment in Meryton. She is astonished to hear that he was the boyhood friend of Mr _____, whose schemings have deprived him of his living.

_____ proposes, but Elizabeth turns him down. Mrs Bennet is furious, but Mr Bennet backs his daughter up. Next thing Elizabeth knows, Collins has proposed to her friend _____ – and been accepted. Meanwhile, _____ has been left depressed by the news that Mr _____ has gone to London and probably won't be back.

Mrs Bennet's brother, Mr _____, and his wife, come to visit. It's agreed that _____ will stay with them in London for a while. On her way to visit _____ and her new husband in Kent, Elizabeth stops off in London to see Jane: her aunt invites her to join herself and Mr Gardiner on a tour of the _____ District the following summer. Charlotte seems content in her new home, absurd as her husband is. Darcy arrives to visit his aunt, Lady _____ de _____. Praising Darcy one day, a cousin of his tells Elizabeth how he saved his friend Bingley from a 'most imprudent marriage'. She is angry to think that this marriage would have been with _____.

_____ proposes to an astonished Elizabeth, who refuses, telling him he has destroyed her sister's happiness, not to mention _____'s prospects. Out walking next day, she is accosted by Darcy, who gives her a letter defending his conduct.

THE STORY OF PRIDE AND PREJUDICE

Back in Hertfordshire her sisters are hoping Mr Bennet will take the family to _____, where the regiment is to be posted. In the event, _____ is invited down by an officer's wife.

Elizabeth sets off with the _____s, though for lack of time they'll only be going to Derbyshire. Elizabeth is appalled when her aunt suggests a sightseeing visit to _____'s house at _____. She is mortified when, walking in the grounds there next day, they meet the owner himself. But he is kind and courteous to Elizabeth and the Gardiners. Next day he brings his party to visit them at the inn: his sister _____ isn't proud, as she has heard: only shy. _____ is as friendly as ever.

Elizabeth hears that _____ has run away to Scotland with _____. _____ arrives to find Elizabeth white with shock: she tells him the whole story and he goes off grim-faced. Back at Longbourn, Jane is holding the fort. Mr _____ persuades Mr Bennet to return home while he hunts for the runaways in London. News comes at last that they have been found and are to be married. The newly-weds visit before heading north to _____ new posting, Lydia letting slip that _____ was at her wedding. Elizabeth writes to ask Mrs _____ what he was doing there, only to be told that it was he who had traced the couple and paid _____ off.

Back now at Netherfield, _____'s feelings for Jane seem undiminished, but Elizabeth cannot interpret _____'s manner. _____ and Jane become engaged. Out of the blue, Lady _____ comes, demanding that Elizabeth promises not to marry _____, which she refuses to do. Some days later, _____ visits with Bingley. He asks Elizabeth if she still feels about him as she did when she rejected him before. No, she replies, she feels completely differently.

now you've got the plot, take a break: there'll be a lot of people to meet in the next section

11

Who's Who

The Mini Mind Map above summarises the main characters in *Pride and Prejudice*. After you have read this chapter test yourself by looking at the full Mind Map on p. 19, and then copying the Mini Mind Map and trying to add to it from memory.

Elizabeth

Clever, independent-minded, lively and loveable, Elizabeth Bennet is an unforgettable heroine. She sets the whole book buzzing with energy. Jane Austen herself considered Lizzy her novel's most important asset. 'I must confess', she wrote modestly in a letter to a friend, 'that I think her as delightful a creature as ever appeared in print.' Delightful she may be, but she has a lot to learn as the novel begins. The *prejudice* of the title is hers, of course. Looking no further than to appearances, she underestimates Darcy's true worth every bit as badly as she overestimates Wickham's. The recognition that she can make mistakes comes hard to a girl who knows she is smart and is used to being right about things: what matters, though, is that she has the capacity to learn by her mistakes – and to grow by doing so.

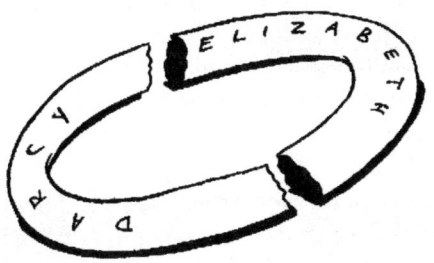

INTROVERT • EXTROVERT

RESERVED • OUTGOING

STEADY • IMPETUOUS

SERIOUS • IRREVERENT

EXPERIENCED • NAÏVE

A marriage of opposites

Darcy

Darcy takes some growing into. Austere and uncompromising, his reputed rudeness can be attributed in part (though not entirely) to shyness. His arrogance, while exaggerated by the envious, is real enough. However, he is capable of recognising faults in himself when he tries. The transformation he makes in response to Elizabeth's rejection will be evident when she meets him at Pemberley in Chapter 43 (*Her astonishment ... was extreme; and continually was she repeating, 'Why is he so altered? From what can it proceed?'*, p. 276). Darcy is a bigger man to start with than Elizabeth assumes; like her, though, he will grow in the course of the novel.

Jane

Beautiful in appearance, Jane is still more beautiful in spirit. Too much so, perhaps: her insistence on giving everybody the benefit of the doubt results in her failure to see through Miss Bingley's strategies, jeopardising not only her own but Bingley's happiness. Her lack of assertiveness means that her opinions tend to go unheard, just as her lack of animation means her feelings are not taken seriously. Hence the misunderstanding Charlotte predicts for her at the start of Chapter 6 – a prediction which is borne out as Elizabeth realises when she thinks about Darcy's letter in Chapter 36 (p. 237).

Mr Bennet

For what do we live, asks Mr Bennet, *but to make sport for our neighbours, and laugh at them in our turn?* (Chapter 57, p. 372). This humorous philosophy is at once Mr Bennet's most appealing feature and the mark of his failure as a father. If his wife is too silly to take serious responsibility for anything; Mr Bennet is too lazy. Having fallen out of love with the wife whose youthful beauty once *captivated* him (Chapter 42, p. 262), he has effectively withdrawn from family life. For his younger daughters, especially, he has been an absent father – though only a room away, shut up in his library. Far from correcting the foibles of the spoiled, silly girls that their mother's upbringing has inevitably produced, Mr Bennet laughs at them, revealing a detachment from the life of his family that is almost neglectful.

Mrs Bennet

Jane Austen sums up Mrs Bennet's character at the end of Chapter 1 (p. 53): *She was a woman of mean understanding, little information, and uncertain temper … The business of her life was to get her daughters married; its solace was visiting and news.* Brought up to be a charming, empty-headed flirt, she remains a silly 16-year-old trapped in a matron's body. Though her folly is often comic, the damage it has done her daughters is immeasurable, for while she is plainly not actively 'evil', her infantile selfishness makes her incapable of serious moral thinking, or personal development. Never herself truly educated, she has not developed either the imagination or the moral discipline to put herself in another's position. So she can in her way be chillingly ruthless. She would be happy, for example, to hand Elizabeth over to a miserable marriage with Mr Collins for the convenience of keeping Longbourn in the family. Just accomplished enough to catch a husband, Mrs Bennet never acquired the rationality required to keep his love or respect. She has passed these limitations on to her younger daughters.

Lydia

Neglected by her father, Lydia has become her mother's daughter, empty-headed and vain. The attentions of officers have convinced her that she is a beauty, though what appeal she has lies not so much in her looks as in her *high animal spirits* (Chapter 9, p. 91). *Sometimes one officer, sometimes another had been her favourite, as their attentions raised them in her opinion* recalls Elizabeth later. *Her affections had been continually fluctuating, but never without an object* (Chapter 46, p. 297). So superficial are her feelings that she cannot maintain an emotional focus – any more than she can listen to anyone for *more than half a minute* (Chapter 39, p. 249). Only the narrowness of her Longbourn existence prevents Lydia from disgracing her family much earlier. Once she slips the leash in Brighton she is out of control.

Mary

At first glance Mary seems to break the mould among the younger Bennet girls. Where they are concerned only with superficialities – clothes and flirtations – she prefers serious matters like music and morality. Her interest in these deep things is shallow, however. She plays the piano mechanically, without the taste or feeling to match her execution (Chapter 6, p. 71), and though she can recite moral quotations by the yard there's no sign that her reading has brought her any more human understanding (Chapter 47, p. 305). Snatching at any opportunity to perform (Chapter 18, p. 142), she is as vain of her imagined accomplishments as Lydia is of her fancied charms.

Kitty

Though not the youngest of the Bennet sisters, Kitty is the least fully formed as a character. A sort of small-time Lydia through much of the novel's action, she is, we are told (Chapter 61, p. 393), later taken in hand by her older sisters, with encouraging results. Jane Austen's implication is clear: with the right sort of guidance from their parents, the younger Bennet girls might all have turned out better.

Bingley

Bingley's character is evident from his first appearance, a *good looking and gentlemanlike* young man, at the Meryton assembly in Chapter 3 (p. 58). He has *easy, unaffected manners*, and where his sisters seem proud and superior and his friend Darcy comes across as being offensively aloof, he himself pitches in, dancing every dance and generally doing his bit to make the evening go with a swing. Bingley's failings are the same as his strengths: the openness and generosity which make him so likeable also make him easily led. He fails either to see through his sisters' scheming or stand up as he should to Darcy's better-intentioned (but still bullying) interference.

Bingley also serves as a bridge between his reserved friend Darcy and the world (Colonel Fitzwilliam will serve a similar function later, when Darcy is at Rosings, Chapters 30–6). Darcy would never have dreamed of going to a Meryton assembly had his friend not dragged him along. He does go, however, and meets Elizabeth. Bingley is a bridge, too, between Darcy and us readers. At a time when we are seeing Darcy only through the unsympathetic eyes of Elizabeth and her circle, the fact that he's Bingley's friend reassures us that he can't be all bad.

Wickham

One has got all the goodness, says Elizabeth comparing Darcy and Wickham once she knows a little more about their respective histories, *and the other all the appearance of it* (Chapter 39, p. 252). Wickham is living proof that pleasing looks are no guarantee of an honest heart. And it is not just a question of looks. Elizabeth responds to his apparent warmth and openness – and he turns out a cunning schemer. Wickham thus confounds Elizabeth's deepest prejudices – but they need confounding. Only when she has understood that the handsome looks and charming manner of Wickham can conceal a vicious user can Elizabeth move on to think more perceptively about Darcy.

WHO'S WHO?

Charlotte

At 27 (Chapter 5, p. 65), Charlotte is Elizabeth's older confidante, her intellectual equal (she has *an excellent understanding*, says Elizabeth, Chapter 32, p. 212) but her temperamental opposite. *I am not romantic* (Chapter 22, p. 165), she tells her horrified friend after accepting Mr Collins, and her outrageously prosaic views on love and marriage can generally be relied on to appal Elizabeth. Yet they are views worth hearing, a challenge not only to Elizabeth's idealism but to our own readerly sense of what is romantically fitting.

Mrs Gardiner

The Gardiners seem to stand in at Pemberley for the proper parents Elizabeth should have had, allowing her to present herself with a dignity which was never possible in Hertfordshire. Yet Mrs Gardiner's position is not quite so simple. *Several years younger than Mrs Bennet* (Chapter 25, p. 127), Mrs Gardiner also serves as a more big-sisterly confidante, a stand-in for Jane or Charlotte. We trust her judgement, so the fact that she finds Wickham persuasive to begin with makes us judge Elizabeth less severely for being taken in. Similarly, when she and her husband meet Darcy at Pemberley (Chapters 43–7), and find him both impressive and likeable, we accept that we are receiving an objective impression of the 'real' Mr Darcy.

Mr Collins

Grotesquely pompous and polite, Collins doesn't merely follow the conventions but almost obsessively draws attention to the fact that he is following them. Any grateful guest might send his or her host a thank-you letter on returning home, but Mr Collins makes a point of telling Mr Bennet that he will be doing that once he gets back from his first visit to Longbourn (Chapter 22, p. 164). In Chapter 14 (p. 111), he boasts: *I sometimes amuse myself with suggesting and arranging such little elegant compliments as may be adapted to ordinary occasions.* Then he adds – quite incredibly in the light of the way he constantly draws attention to his own courtesies – *I always wish to give them as unstudied an air as possible.*

A classic comic creation, Mr Collins also serves a more serious function in the novel: he highlights with his ridiculous politeness the extent to which normal consideration and friendliness between people can be turned into an empty parody by genteel manners and 'etiquette'.

Lady Catherine

Mr Collins's other important function, of course, is as courtier in chief to Lady Catherine de Bourgh. His grovelling civility complements her insufferable arrogance. Both of them caricature the more absurd aspects of the English class system. His elaborate flattery illustrates the empty shell to which 'courtesy' can be reduced. Her haughtiness underlines the meaninglessness of rank where it is not accompanied by real worth. Lady Catherine assumes that her exalted birth entitles her to probe into everybody else's business. It is ironic, though, that such a grand lady can find nothing more important to do than persecuting the poor of her parish over their pettiest offences (Chapter 30, p. 203) and criticising the domestic management of her more genteel acquaintances.

But if Lady Catherine is a highly objectionable character, she is also – despite herself – an important one. It may be a mark of personal inadequacy that she likes to make herself feel superior by surrounding herself with her obvious social inferiors, but her condescension is crucial to the structuring of the novel. It is because of it, for instance, that the company from Hunsford Parsonage gets its invitation to dinner at Rosings, where Elizabeth will so impress Darcy in Chapter 31. Similarly, Lady Catherine's attempt to bully Elizabeth into promising not to marry Darcy (Chapter 56) is the catalyst for his second proposal, convincing him that Elizabeth may not after all be entirely hostile towards him. One of the things that makes a novel compelling is when its characters are real enough to convince us as people. Reading more critically, though, we can see that, in addition to being creations in their own right, they serve a function in the mechanics of the action.

now you know who's who, take another break before moving on to what's what with a look at Jane Austen's themes

WHO'S WHO?

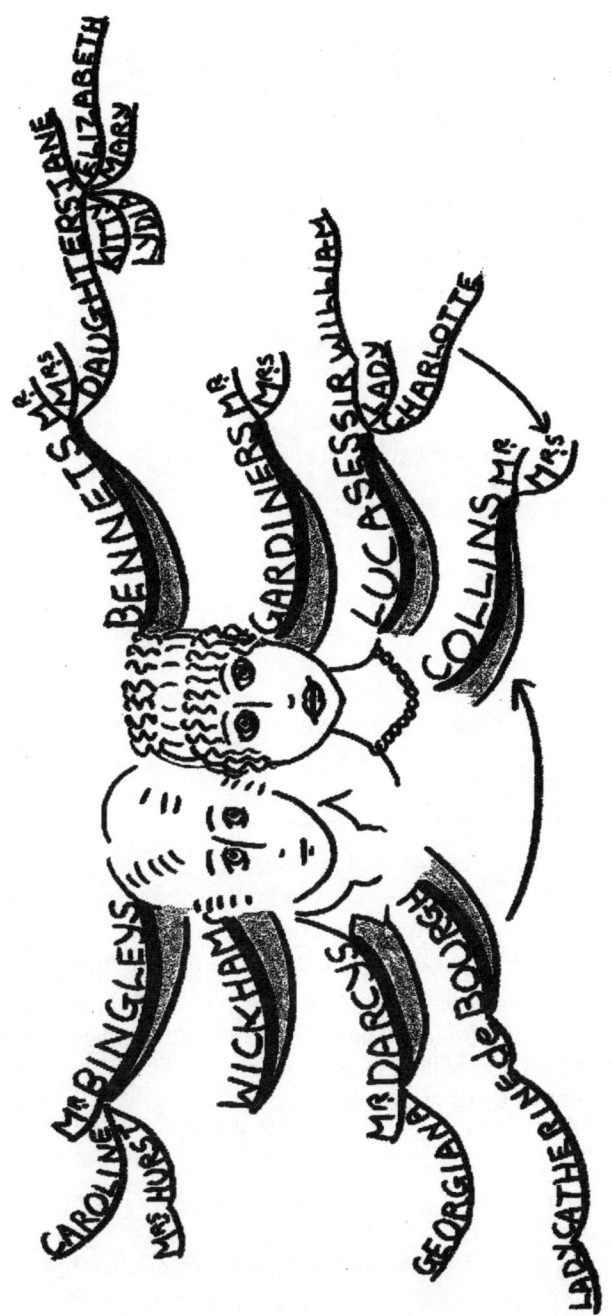

Themes

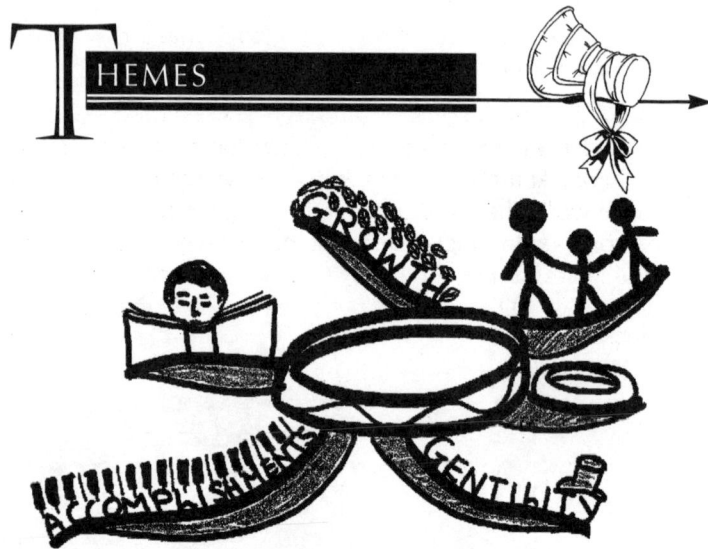

A **theme** is an idea developed or explored throughout a work. The main themes of *Pride and Prejudice* are shown in the Mini Mind Map above. 'Imagery' refers to the kind of word picture used to bring the themes to life. Test yourself on the themes by copying the Mini Mind Map, adding to it yourself, and then comparing your results with the full Mind Map on p. 27.

Family

Jane Austen believes that family life is fundamental. Which is not the same as saying that she thinks it's necessarily a good thing. Our family background is one of the things that make us what we are. We may maintain, as in Jane Austen's day the Romantic poets and philosophers did, that we are individuals first and last; that we can in a sense be what we want to be, re-creating ourselves by sheer effort of will. But it's not quite so easy, says *Pride and Prejudice*: the individual inhabits, inescapably, a wider social context and the family is the (often troubled) point at which the individual and that context meet.

Idealist that she is, Elizabeth starts out by imagining that she and her sensible sister Jane can rise above a silly family. As the novel goes on, however, it becomes clear that their mother's and sisters' folly and their father's irresponsibility are going to haunt them wherever they go. They cannot as individuals leave their backgrounds behind.

Morally, of course, they may do so – indeed must – and for us as readers the happy endings to their romances are a reward for effort. At the same time, however, we see that in the real, social world the sisters inhabit they depend for their fortunate outcome upon Bingley's easy-going readiness to overlook Jane's background and Darcy's resolution in conquering his reservations. Darcy would not of course have managed this if Elizabeth's own strength of character had not acted upon him to strengthen *his* resolve. The fact remains, though, that he cannot have an Elizabeth detached from her background, but must accept her, family and all. The way he assumes responsibility for dealing with Lydia's elopement represents his recognition of this.

Marriage

Marriage is a central theme of *Pride and Prejudice*. Though she holds it out as the 'happy ending' for Elizabeth and Jane's respective romances, Jane Austen does not let us settle for such a rosy view. Several marriages are presented in the novel, with various problems. Mr and Mrs Gardiner's may be a model partnership – rational, responsible, loving and companionable – but the overall tone is set by life at Longbourn. In Mr and Mrs Bennet's marriage, the lack of equality, and of shared interests, sympathies or mutual respect, has damaged not only husband and wife but their children too.

A MARRIAGE OF CONVENIENCE

Charlotte Lucas and Collins's marriage is one of economic survival for her, and form for him. She marries him because, *Without thinking highly either of men or of matrimony, marriage had always been her object; it was the only honourable provision for well-educated young women of small fortune, and however uncertain of giving happiness, must be their pleasantest preservative from want* (Chapter 22, p. 163); he marries her because his patroness considers it fitting for a clergyman to have a wife (Chapter 19, p. 147).

Lydia and Wickham's marriage is, of course, a disaster for her family. If it does not make Lydia herself as wretched as we might have expected, this is only because she is too silly to sense the degradation in a life's partnership with a liar and a seducer who has had to be paid to stand by her.

A PERFECT MATCH

Marriage in *Pride and Prejudice* is also, however, a starting-point from which we can examine how human relationships work more generally. For Jane Austen, it seems, each party's strengths and weaknesses must correct and compensate for those of the other. In looking for friends or lovers, we shouldn't be looking for people exactly like us but for people whose different characters complement our own. We see this in Elizabeth and Jane's close relationship as sisters, in which Elizabeth's animation and outgoingness are balanced by Jane's quieter reflectiveness. We see it, too, in Darcy's friendship with Bingley (See Jane Austen's comments on this, Chapter 4, p. 64). But the subject is explored most fully in the relationship between Elizabeth and Darcy. Their whole story can be seen in terms of Elizabeth's long, difficult journey to realising that his very differences from her are what make Darcy *exactly the man, who, in disposition and talents, would most suit her* (Chapter 50, p. 325).

Gentility

All the main characters of *Pride and Prejudice* are, broadly speaking, genteel. Jane Austen, however, is interested in looking beyond this to question just what it is that makes a true gentleman or lady. Social rank and wealth must be a part of it – but not, judging by the example of Lady Catherine de Bourgh, the whole. Manners are obviously important – but are we really to believe that Mr Collins's elaborate obsequiousness makes him more gentlemanly than the reserved – some would say rude – Mr Darcy? Elizabeth's *low connections* are, says Darcy (Chapter 8, p. 82) a handicap to her marrying a man *of any consideration in the world*, yet he himself will find the impropriety of her relations' behaviour a stronger objection

THEMES

than this accident of birth. Meeting at Pemberley (Chapter 43), he will greet the Gardiners – a London lawyer and his wife – with courtesy and warmth; later, after Lydia's elopment, he will feel more comfortable dealing with Mr Gardiner than with the higher-born Mr Bennet (Chapter 52, p. 336). It would be foolish to deny the importance of money and social rank, implies Jane Austen – but what matters most is personal worth.

Accomplishments

In Jane Austen's day, every young girl with any claim to gentility had to apply herself to the task of acquiring *accomplishments* – that set of skills and knowledge which she would need to have if she were to attract the right sort of gentleman. Music, drawing, needlework, languages: these are all marvellous skills to have – sources, potentially, of great enjoyment, insight and creativity. Young Georgiana Darcy, it's clear (Chapter 43), practises all day long through sheer love of her music, finding in it not only an obvious delight but also, perhaps, an outlet for feelings she cannot otherwise express. No mere ornament, music is a key to Georgiana's personal depth and creativity.

By and large, though, Jane Austen seems to feel that young ladies worked at such accomplishments not in a spirit of creative enthusiasm but grudgingly, as the necessary price of a good marriage. Like a fine dress or a fashionable hairdo, skill with a needle or at the keyboard might 'set off' the young lady to her best advantage, helping her to attract a wealthy husband. But how much did she really get out of them for herself? And how far would they equip her for the ordinary challenges of adult life? How far, in other words, should we see this sort of 'accomplishment' as representing what we would consider genuine 'education'?

AN UNATTAINABLE IDEAL

An informal debate among the company at Netherfield (Chapter 8, pp. 84–5) reveals some disagreement about what constitutes the 'accomplished' woman. Bingley's snobbish sisters clearly think accomplishment is about surface elegance and fashionable display, while Darcy thinks something more is required (something so much more, including extensive and serious reading on top of all the more usual things, that Elizabeth regards it as an unattainable ideal).

Whether or not every young girl has to be the sort of dedicated scholar that Darcy seems to want, it is plain that, for Jane Austen, superficial 'accomplishments' are no substitute for real education. Mrs Bennet's upbringing made her a captivating bride but a hopeless wife and mother. The silly female characters who abound in Jane Austen's fiction testify not to her contempt for her own sex but to her indignant consciousness of how her fellow women were being let down. Her society, she felt, wanted women to be attractive, elegant and ornamental – rather than capable of serious, independent thought. Yet faced with life's problems, women have to be able to make intelligent judgements just as men do. The woman whose upbringing has left her unable to think properly suffers a severe handicap. Look at the damage Mrs Bennet's foolishness does to her family; look at her daughter Lydia – a vain, undisciplined accident waiting to happen.

Reading

Time and again we find when we're reading *Pride and Prejudice* that its characters seem to be reading too: many of the novel's most important developments or revelations come through letters, which their recipients then have to read and interpret. In Chapter 21 (p. 159), for instance, Elizabeth and Jane go over Caroline Bingley's letter with a fine-toothed comb, trying to establish the meaning both in and between the lines. Darcy's letter in Chapter 35 will turn Elizabeth's life upside-down, while Jane's letters in Chapter 46, bringing the news of Lydia's elopement, will seem to dash hopes Elizabeth hasn't till that moment fully realised she has.

INTERPRETATION

But reading isn't only about words on a page. Elizabeth tends to replay every important incident, every conversation, in her mind afterwards, trying to work out the significance of every word, every deed, every gesture and expression. Often she will discuss her reading with Jane or Charlotte – and often they will

THEMES

disagree, for every text has a number of possible interpretations. Elizabeth's reading of Wickham's character as an amiable and ill-used man seems the only possible interpretation – until Darcy's letter suggests another, quite different, one.

This is what Mary fails to see, despite reading more, and more seriously, than anyone else in the novel. She reads without learning because she reads literally. She has not understood what Jane Austen makes very clear to us in our reading of *Pride and Prejudice*: reading is not a passive process of downloading words; we must actively, energetically *interpret* what is written. And we must recall, too, that each text has many possible readings. Elizabeth will learn this to her cost. At least, though, she will be capable of learning – of revising, readjusting her views in the light of new interpretations, new insights. That is what will enable her to grow.

Growth

Elizabeth gets older in the course of *Pride and Prejudice*, but she also grows up. The two things are not the same. Elizabeth's mother and father both seem stuck in timeless, changeless routines – her mother busy to no purpose about her endless round of visiting, fussing and complaining, her father hidden away in his library. Mrs Bennet is too silly even to engage with real experience. Look at her delighted reaction to Lydia's wedding (Chapter 49), for instance: she is lost in a world of her own, so silly it's a sort of mild insanity. Mr Bennet for his part is highly intelligent – but too morally lazy to put himself to the trouble of taking life seriously. Both seem infantile in their cheerful irresponsibility, their ready acceptance of a life without challenges.

Elizabeth, on the other hand, seems grown up. In the absence of any sensible parenting, she and her sister Jane have become their younger sisters' effective guardians. But she feels increasingly fretful within the narrow horizons of her Longbourn life, her dissatisfaction itself a sign that she is outgrowing her childhood home, hungry for new experiences. These will come with the arrival of Bingley and his guests – notably, of course, Darcy. Wickham will appear with his winning ways and his hard-luck story. She will travel – to Kent and to Derbyshire.

Jane and Elizabeth step into a bigger world than they are used to, and a rougher one: for Jane there is the pain of love's loss; for Elizabeth the ill-concealed hostility of Miss Bingley, the offensive attentions of Mr Collins, the insulting condescension of Lady Catherine – and of course the perplexing behaviour of Mr Darcy. There will be mistakes and misunderstandings, utter confusion for a girl accustomed to feeling competent.

Elizabeth and Darcy's romance will be a learning process for both – painful and at times humiliating. In coming to see the hidden depths in Darcy's character, Elizabeth will have to face the hidden superficialities in her own judgement. In recognising Elizabeth's worth, Darcy will have to recognise the limits of his own. In changing their view of each other, they will be changing themselves, and growing.

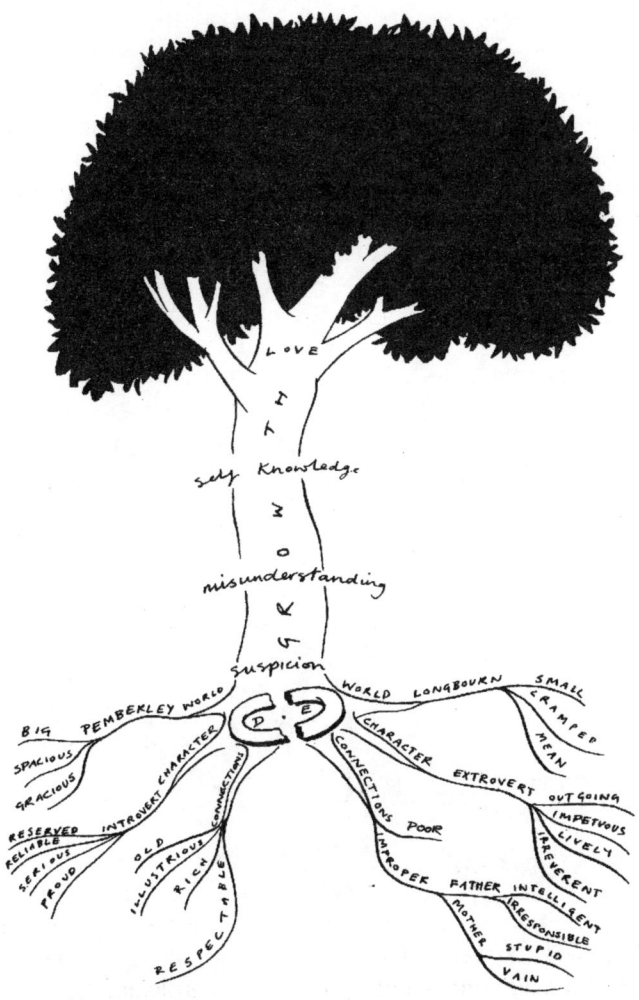

The roots of happiness

time for a change for you too: take a good look at the Mind Map (on the next page) summarising the themes then do something else for a while before moving on to the Commentary

PRIDE AND PREJUDICE

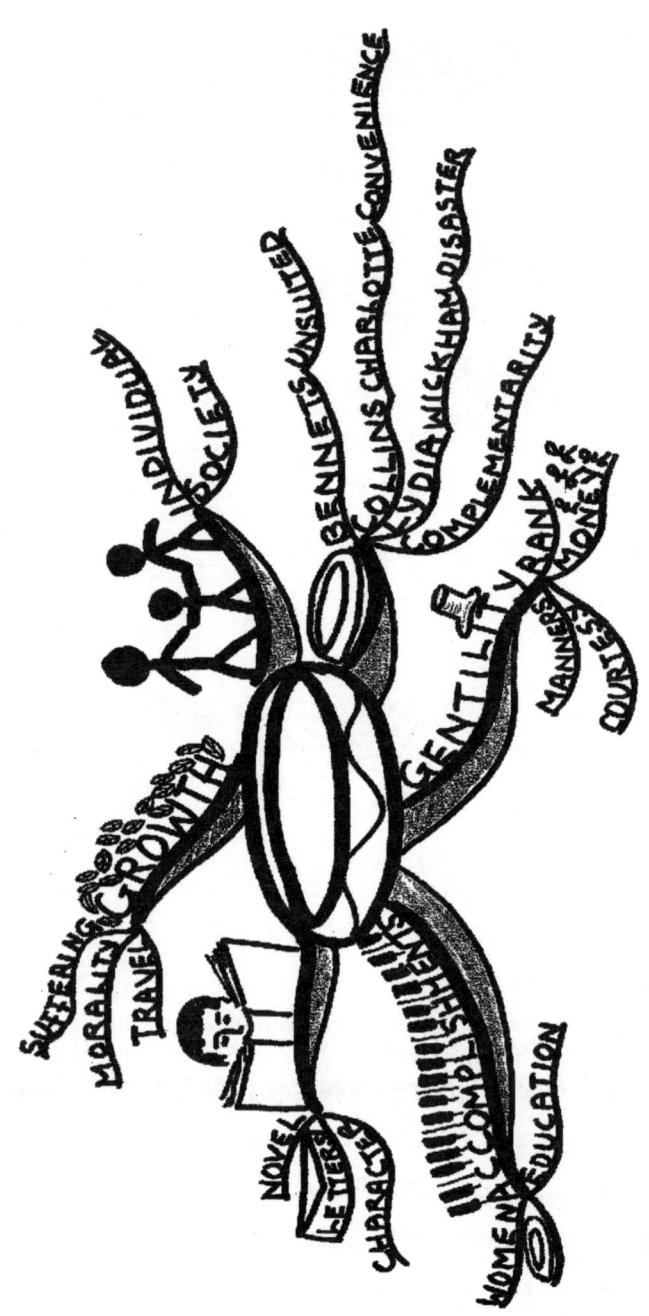

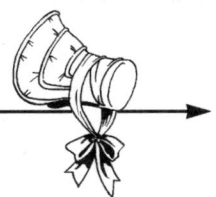

The Commentary divides the chapters into short sections, beginning with a brief preview which will prepare you for the section and help with last-minute revision. The Commentary comments on whatever is important in the section, focusing on the areas shown in the Mini Mind Map above.

Wherever there is a focus on a particular theme, the icon for that theme appears in the margin (see p. x for key). Look out, too, for the 'Style and language' sections. Being able to comment on style and language will help you to get an 'A' in your exam.

USE YOUR NOVEL

You will learn more from the Commentary if you use it alongside the novel itself. Read a section from the novel, then the corresponding Commentary section – or the other way around.

Remember that when a question appears in the Commentary with a star ✪ in front of it, you should stop and think about it for a moment. And **remember** to take a break after completing each exercise!

PRIDE AND PREJUDICE

Chapters 1–6, *Longbourn meets Netherfield*

- ◆ Mr Bingley moves into Netherfield Hall.
- ◆ He seems a nice young man.
- ◆ His friend Mr Darcy isn't so likeable.

The first people we meet are not Jane and Elizabeth but their parents. They don't seem such a great advertisement for love or marriage. It is an odd way, when you think about it, to open what we assume is to be a novel of romantic love!

In Mr and Mrs Bennet's conversation, Jane Austen sketches in some essential background efficiently and enjoyably. We find out that the sisters have complementary qualities; that Jane is the beauty and that Elizabeth has 'quickness'. We notice almost immediately that the Bennets don't agree on how to treat their daughters, and wonder what effect this has on the girls. Do they see their parents' incompatibility? Mrs Bennet's stupidity is obvious, but is her husband really so preferable? From their opening exchange we see Mrs Bennet making a fool of herself and her husband, with something close to sadism, encouraging her to. As we enjoy the dazzling humour of Chapter 1, we gradually sense the misery it must be masking. We may even feel a bit guilty: having enjoyed Mr Bennet's jokes, it's as if we've given his attitude our approval.

Reader's rights?

Jane Austen throws us off our guard, making us question the way we are reading her novel. As readers we expect to be given the story 'straight'. We feel we have a deal with the author: we'll accept your story; you play fair with us. From the first, *Pride and Prejudice* refuses to go along with this cosy contract. It assumes that, in reading as in life, appearances may mislead; we make mistakes and have to revise our views. What are we to make of this book? Is it a brilliant comedy? No question. Is it a work of seriousness, even sadness? Well, yes, that too. The same scene can be read in very different ways.

The arrival of a new neighbour is a big event for a family whose existence has been very narrow. While Lydia and Kitty hope for dances and entertainments, even their more

COMMENTARY

serious sisters Jane and Elizabeth are curious about the newcomer. The withdrawal of their father from family life; the folly of their mother and younger sisters, leave Jane and Elizabeth with only each other, within the family, for companionship. The routine is established and unchanging: their father shut away in his library, their mother busy to no purpose about her daily round of visiting. There's no future for them here: Jane and Elizabeth are outgrowing Longbourn and looking to the world beyond.

AN INVASION OF LIFE

Yet with the arrival of the regiment at Meryton and the coming of Bingley and his party to Netherfield that world suddenly seems to be beating a path to their door. There is of course another side to this sudden broadening of horizons. If the sisters have had a narrow existence, it has been in many ways a protected one; if life at Longbourn has been static – even stagnant – it has also been reassuringly stable. Now, we sense, things are about to change. Is the Bennet family going to be strong enough to cope? Will Elizabeth and Jane be able to carve out their own individual destinies?

A rumour before he's ever a fact, Bingley doesn't become a reality until Chapter 3. *Good-looking and gentlemanlike*, with *a pleasant countenance, and easy, unaffected manners*, Bingley is all that the girls have hoped, even obliging Mrs Bennet by taking to Jane! His sisters are ominously intimidating, though, with their *air of decided fashion* (Chapter 3, p. 58). Rumour flourishes at the gathering, the buzz going round first about Darcy's handsomeness, his abilities, his fortune – then about the 'fact' that *He was the proudest, most disagreeable man in the world*. He isn't as easy and open a character as Bingley, yet there's a hint of hidden depths. Men and women alike think him handsome (Chapter 3, p. 58), suggesting a complex figure who can be seen in a number of different ways.

MEET ELIZABETH BENNET

This is also our first introduction to Elizabeth in person. Our meeting with her coincides with her meeting with Darcy – or, rather, with her failure to meet him (Chapter 3, p. 58). This

A false start is appropriate for a relationship which is to be marked so badly by misunderstanding. But there's no misunderstanding about Darcy's ungraciousness here. Though silly things are said about his supposed rudeness, he *is* rather rude about Elizabeth (*She is tolerable; but not handsome enough to tempt me*)! She isn't pleased, of course, but instead of resenting his offensiveness she is able to make a joke of it. Elizabeth may be the social 'inferior' in this encounter, but her grace brings her out the clear winner as far as the reader is concerned.

It is noticeable as we go through the book that every gathering, every important conversation, every letter becomes – like your copy of *Pride and Prejudice* – a text for study. Much of Jane and Elizabeth's closeness is formed by such conversations. They talk about a scene they have just witnessed as if it were a scene in a novel each has read. The same text can be read very differently, though, according to who is reading it.

Chapter 4 shows us two separate accounts of the same social gathering, two attempts by different groups of participants to 'read' a scene we ourselves have just participated in as readers. And if this particular scene has been interpreted very differently by the Longbourn and Netherfield groups, there are differences, too, in Jane and Elizabeth's readings of events. Jane's view that the Bingley sisters are *very pleasing women when you converse with them* and that Caroline Bingley will prove a *charming neighbour* is not shared by Elizabeth. Which view is nearer to the truth will become clear immediately afterwards, when we see Bingley and his party in conversation at Netherfield. While they judge the Bennet girls, we are judging *them*!

COMPLEMENTARY CHARACTERS

The relationship between Mr and Mrs Bennet has already illustrated the problems there can be when a husband and wife have nothing in common. But Jane Austen asks us to consider whether, for all that, differences may not be essential to good relationships. In Chapter 4 we see first the closeness Jane and Elizabeth have achieved despite their

COMMENTARY

temperamental differences. Then, only moments later (Chapter 4, p. 64), we see how Bingley and Darcy have *a very steady friendship, in spite of a great opposition of character*). The qualities and shortcomings of each offset those of the other.

By now we're already beginning to feel we know the characters better than they know themselves. Whose openness might offset Darcy's reserve? Who might challenge him the way he clearly needs to be challenged? Whatever they themselves may think, we readers already suspect that Elizabeth and Darcy might be meant for one another.

Chapter 5 offers us another attempt to re-read the scene we saw in the Assembly Rooms in Chapter 3, this time with Mrs Bennet and the Lucases contributing their interpretations. At 27, some years older than the Bennet girls (Jane is 23, Elizabeth 20), Charlotte Lucas is a realist, where Elizabeth tends towards idealism. Free of self-delusion, she accepts without bitterness that Bingley prefers dancing with Jane (Chapter 5, p. 65). Her view of Darcy is worth having, as are her observations on Jane near the start of Chapter 6 (pp. 68–9). Her view that Jane should communicate her feelings to Bingley by what sounds almost like a deliberate strategy of acting strikes the romantic Elizabeth as terribly calculating. She will recall Charlotte's words later, though, in Chapter 35, when she finds that Jane's impassive expression appears indeed to have cost her the man she loves. Darcy will find Elizabeth's face far more informative when he studies her later in the chapter (Chapter 6, p. 70). The face which in Chapter 3 he found only *tolerable* (p. 59) now seems beautiful, but in its animation, its expression. Where Jane's beauty is physical, even sculptural, Elizabeth's face is the window to her mind and personality.

Charlotte also offends Elizabeth with her view of marriage (*Happiness in marriage is entirely a matter of chance* ..., Chapter 6, pp. 69–70). Such cynicism is alien to Elizabeth, whose developing love for Darcy is to be a tale of two strangers who at first dislike each other and then get to know each other well enough to learn how well suited they are. There's just enough truth in what Charlotte says to shake our belief in love stories, though. If the main narrative of *Pride*

33

and Prejudice is to be an exhilarating romance, it is hedged round with more sobering stories: those of the Bennet parents, of Wickham's various conquests, and of course of Charlotte herself.

Test yourself

- ? Name two things which change in the life of Longbourn and surrounding neighbourhood in these early chapters. (See end of test for answer.)
- ? Why does Mrs Bennet want Mr Bennet to visit Mr Bingley on his arrival in the neighbourhood? (See end of test for answer.)
- ? Jane and Elizabeth are 'complementary' characters: their differences are what bring them together. Dividing your page into two columns, with Jane to one side and Elizabeth to the other, try to list some opposites. Jane is passive, for instance, where Elizabeth tends to be active. Can you come up with three more pairings?
- ? Do you think the Bennets are a happy family? Make a Mini Mind Map of your reasons.
- ? How do the different members of the Bennet family like to spend their time? Elizabeth, for instance, likes to read, to walk and to talk about things with Jane. What does Mr Bennet do? Mrs Bennet? Lydia? And how about Mary?
- ? What actions in these first few chapters have shown Elizabeth to be lively and spirited?

ANSWERS

Things which have changed in the life of Longbourn include the arrival in the neighbourhood of Bingley, Darcy, and the rest of their party, and the posting of the regiment to Meryton.

Mr Bennet is to visit Mr Bingley so that Mr Bingley can invite the rest of the family over and fall in love with one of her daughters.

now take a break: next stop Netherfield

COMMENTARY

Chapters 7–12, *Elizabeth at Netherfield*

- Jane falls ill during a visit to Netherfield.
- Elizabeth goes to keep her company.
- Darcy is obviously attracted to her; Miss Bingley isn't pleased.

Chapter 7 opens with some bald facts about the Bennet family. In the absence of a male heir, Mr Bennet's property won't come down to his daughters. Mrs Bennet, it seems, comes from a lower *station in life*. The novel's early chapters have allowed us to get to know Elizabeth and Jane a little as personalities. But sordid as it may seem, they are defined not only by their characters but by their social position and fortune. There are bottom lines in the matter, as revealed here – and underscored a little later, in Chapter 8, pp. 82–3, where the Bennet girls' uncle in Cheapside comes up for discussion among Bingley's party. The scorn of Bingley's sisters is neither here nor there – we've already seen how shallow their claims to rank really are (*their brother's fortune and their own had been acquired by trade*, Jane Austen tells us damningly in Chapter 4, p. 63). But Darcy is the real thing, and doesn't take Bingley's light view of the matter. The other problem with Elizabeth's family is its behaviour. The arrival of the militia in Meryton will of course bring out the worst in her mother and younger sisters.

NATURE'S CHILD

Elizabeth's outdoorsy vigour and animation appear as she walks to see her sister at Netherfield (Chapter 7, p. 79), *crossing field after field at a quick pace, jumping over stiles and springing over puddles with impatient activity, and finding herself at last within view of the house, with weary ancles, dirty stockings, and a face glowing with the warmth of exercise*. There is much sheer snobbery in Bingley's sisters' apparent contempt for someone who doesn't go everywhere by carriage. But they also object because they sense that what Mrs Hurst will describe as Elizabeth's *almost wild* appearance after her walk (Chapter 8, p. 81) shows off to its best advantage a beauty which, as we saw in Chapter 6, is to be seen not in Elizabeth's still face and figure but in animation and movement.

35

> 🎗 Elizabeth has never been the subject of this sort of scrutiny before, whether the admiring looks of the gentlemen or the ladies' critical dissection. We saw at the start of this section that Elizabeth and Jane are defined not only by their own characters but by their family's circumstances. Sheltered as her upbringing has been, however, it is only now, as she steps out of her familiar Longbourn circle and into the wider world represented by Netherfield, that Elizabeth is beginning to realise this. Hence the physical symptoms of her shame when her mother comes to Netherfield. Squirming with embarrassment, she finds herself *blushing* (Chapter 9, p. 89) and feels herself *tremble* (p. 90). This scene is almost too cringeworthy to be comic.

Caroline Bingley's attempt at the end of Chapter 10 to freeze Elizabeth out of the company while walking in the grounds is the culmination of a long series of slights and insults but, like all the others, it backfires on her. This Netherfield visit is the first of three extended stays Elizabeth has away from Longbourn: Netherfield, Kent and Pemberley. Here (where of course she hasn't even been officially invited, having come just to keep her sick sister company) Elizabeth is so far from being on home ground that she is actually under attack. But she survives – even shines – triumphing over their rudeness as we saw her triumphing over Darcy's first unthinking remark in Chapter 3. Far from destroying her in Darcy's sight, Caroline Bingley's antagonistic remarks have only shown Elizabeth off to best advantage. Even so, this scene in the shrubbery represents some kind of climax. Elizabeth is physically squeezed out by Bingley's sisters: where is their breeding now? But though Darcy intervenes, Elizabeth has no need of his help: unintimidated, independent, her own woman, she cuts a more impressive figure than ever as she trots cheerfully off alone.

PRIDE

Chapter 11 brings a discussion of whether pride should be considered a weakness. Darcy's is, of course, the *pride* of the novel's title, where *prejudice* is Elizabeth's vice. Here, however, he remains proud of his pride. Ironically enough, he makes the sort of *indirect boast* he criticised Bingley for earlier

COMMENTARY

(Chapter 10, p. 93), complimenting himself on his uncompromising firmness under cover of regretting his unyieldingness. Elizabeth calls his bluff, though, telling him he has every reason to feel guilty about a failing such as this.

Returning to Longbourn in Chapter 12, Elizabeth and Jane find the family home reduced by their absence (*The evening conversation ... had lost much of its animation*, Chapter 12, p. 105). Mary, who has been *deep in the study of ... human nature*, has *some new observations of thread-bare morality* with which to regale them. After dealing with real-life human nature during her stay at Netherfield – riding out Caroline Bingley's hostility and sparring with Darcy – life at Longbourn seems quieter, narrower than ever.

Over to you

- In your own words, what does the 'entailment' entail?
- Why does Mrs Bennet insist that Jane ride over to dine at Netherfield (Chapter 7), rather than travel in the carriage?
- Like Jane and Elizabeth, Bingley and Darcy can be seen as complementary characters. Making two columns, as you did for the two sisters earlier, can you think of three pairs of complementary characteristics for the two young men?
- Look at Chapter 10: Caroline Bingley, we are told, *often tried to provoke Darcy into disliking her guest*: how does she try to do this? And what does this behaviour tell us about her?
- In Chapter 9, after telling Elizabeth not to *run on* for making a perfectly intelligent comment, Mrs Bennet goes on herself to give a virtuoso display of stupidity and rudeness. Some things she says are simply silly – can you find three? Others are more personally unpleasant, though: try to find two of these.

there's a longish haul at Longbourn coming next, so take a quick break

Chapters 13–21, *Mr Collins and Mr Wickham*

- ◆ Two more men arrive in the neighbourhood: the ridiculous Mr Collins and the dashing Mr Wickham.
- ◆ Elizabeth is attracted to the latter, but it's the former who proposes.
- ◆ She turns him down: her mother is furious but her father backs her up.

Mr Collins ushers in the next phase of book. Apart from his obvious comic qualities, Mr Collins is also significant as the relation on which Longbourn is 'entailed'. The entailment, though a practical problem, also plays a symbolic role. We have already seen that Elizabeth is outgrowing her Longbourn life. The entailment means that there is, quite literally, no future for her here. She is going to have to move on.

A SMOOTH TALKER

It's easy to see how attractive Wickham would seem to a girl who has been on the receiving end of Collins's elephantine gallantries. But Wickham is appealing in his own right, with (as his conversation in Chapter 16 amply shows) an instinctive intelligence about people. He certainly sees Elizabeth coming. His casting of Darcy as a rich, selfish and manipulative abuser of his own rank and wealth is exactly what Elizabeth wants to hear about a man whose pride has made her feel small. But Wickham is false in everything he says. He doesn't play whist, he says austerely (Chapter 16, p. 120), but we find out later that he's an incorrigible gambler. Nor does his professed ambition to be a country parson ring any more true in the light of later events.

Notice he doesn't venture a word about Darcy until he's had a clue to Elizabeth's own feelings (Chapter 16, p. 121). Once she has made her prejudices clear, however, he plays on them with the utmost skill: *I have no right to give my opinion* on Darcy's character, he says scrupulously (Chapter 16, p. 121), before embarking on an extended critique. For the sake of the elder Mr Darcy he won't expose the younger's wrongdoings, he insists piously (Chapter 16, p. 123), before blackening his character completely. *It gives me pain to speak ill of a Darcy,* he says (Chapter 16, p. 125), when there is clearly nothing in the world he likes better.

If it seems odd that Elizabeth should allow herself to be fooled so easily, she is of course still reeling from the impact of Collins's attentions – and, perhaps, more affected than she has acknowledged to herself by Darcy's disdain. The venue for the meeting at Aunt Philips's doesn't help, either. She is as irresponsible a guardian as Mrs Bennet, and her home is the scene for much of Lydia and Kitty's frivolity. Elizabeth is lulled into a major error of judgement by the relaxed atmosphere. On top of all that, though, there's the fact that Elizabeth is still young and inexperienced in the ways of the world.

THE NETHERFIELD BALL

The Netherfield ball in Chapter 18 is perhaps the biggest formal social gathering in a novel which can for much of its length be seen as proceeding in a series of social gatherings. An event like this brings people together, and their interactions provide a sort of chemical reaction to drive the action on to the next stage. The ball isn't all Elizabeth had hoped. Despite his earlier insistence (Chapter 16, p. 122) that he has no reason to avoid Darcy's company, Wickham has given the event a miss. We wonder why, even if Elizabeth doesn't. Her preoccupation is not profound, though, and she soon cheers up (Chapter 18, p. 132) – only to find herself suffering two *dances of mortification* with Collins (Chapter 18, p. 132). His appalling dancing underlines his unfitness as Elizabeth's husband, and she experiences the shame of being with him physically – her embarrassment almost tangible, her release an *ecstacy*.

In a daze she accepts a dance with Darcy *without knowing what she did*: a certain spontaneity, even an inevitability, seems to be creeping into her relationship with this young man, however negatively she may think she feels about him. Just as she was brought low by her association with Collins on the dance floor, dancing with Darcy seems to elevate her (her neighbours look at her in *amazement*, Chapter 18, p. 133). Again, whatever Elizabeth may think she thinks of Darcy, she looks right with him; they make a handsome couple. Their conversation is strained and their parting unsatisfactory, but if

Elizabeth is more than ever convinced of her dislike for Darcy, we as readers are surer than ever that they're meant for each other.

If Elizabeth finds it impossible to read anything but honesty in Wickham's pleasant face and manner, the alternative interpretations she is offered all seem to her to be unreliable. Darcy is Wickham's open enemy, of course, while Caroline Bingley, who also in her way attempts to warn her (Chapter 18, pp. 136–7), has her own motives for doing so — and her own objections to Wickham. Mostly seeming to centre on his low birth, they only put Elizabeth's back up. She herself has suffered already from Miss Bingley's snobbery – and more important, from what she takes to be Darcy's. Jane, too, attempts to warn her (Chapter 18, p. 138), but Elizabeth, much as she loves her sister, is accustomed to discounting her testimony. Jane, she assumes, is too kind-hearted to be a reliable witness. The difficulties we have in knowing how to interpret what our fellow men and women say, and what motivates them, is one preoccupation of *Pride and Prejudice*. Only when she has the wisdom to see Wickham's true worthlessness will Elizabeth be capable of appreciating Darcy's worth.

As the evening goes on, Elizabeth finds herself let down by her family. Again, the effects are all but physical. As her mother discourses upon Jane's supposedly forthcoming marriage to Mr Bingley, in Mr Darcy's hearing, Elizabeth blushes repeatedly *with shame and vexation* (Chapter 18, p. 141). She keeps looking to see Darcy's reaction: much as she thinks she dislikes him, his opinion is obviously important to her. She listens *in agonies* as Mary outstays her welcome at the piano (Chapter 18, p. 142), while Collins crowns her humiliation with his pompous speech about music (Chapter 18, pp. 142–3).

MR COLLINS MAKES AN OFFER

Mr Collins's proposal (Chapter 19) is a masterpiece of comic writing, revealing Collins at his most absurd, but showing too a nastier streak beneath the surface. His modesty (*May I hope, Madam...*, Chapter 19, p. 146) is shown to be false (Chapter

COMMENTARY

19, pp. 149–50) when he makes it clear that he considers he has made Elizabeth an offer she cannot refuse, poor as her situation is. He makes great play of saying that money doesn't matter to him, but he has obviously researched her *one thousand pounds in the 4 per cents* (Chapter 19, p. 148). No ungenerous rebuke about her poverty will be made *when we are married*, he assures her – taking it as read that she will accept him.

A scrupulous observer of social conventions, Collins does make some slight show of romantic ardour. *Almost as soon as I entered the house*, he says (and *almost* is right, of course: first he assumed he would be taking Jane!), *I singled you out as the companion of my future life*. His fear that he might be *run away with by my feelings* is priceless. His revelation (Chapter 19, p. 147) that Lady Catherine has instructed him to find a wife is as unromantic as it is unsurprising. Funny as the scene is, however, it is an excruciating experience for Elizabeth. Collins's patronising refusal to take her refusal at face value is of course the ultimate insult. He literally cannot believe that she could refuse him. What makes his complacent speech so chilling, though, is the obvious element of truth in his hint that *it is by no means certain that another offer of marriage may ever be made you. Your portion is unhappily so small …*

A LETTER FROM MISS BINGLEY

What think you of this sentence, my dear Lizzy? Jane and Elizabeth discuss Caroline Bingley's letter (Chapter 21, p. 159) very carefully, sentence by sentence, hoping to work out the motivation that lies behind it. They want to know what, precisely, it means. Jane, a naive literalist, takes it at face value and accepts, however unhappily, that Bingley is destined for Georgiana. *Can there be any other opinion on the subject?* she asks. Of course there can – any text, any speech, any gesture or facial expression can, as we have seen, have a number of different interpretations. Elizabeth, a more penetrating critic, promptly offers a more sceptical reading.

Your turn

- Why is Mr Bennet looking forward to meeting Mr Collins? What are Mrs Bennet's hopes from him?
- Find two phrases in Chapter 15 to show why Jane Austen does not think the reader should have too much respect for Mr Collins.
- What clues does Jane Austen give us that Wickham may not be all he seems?
- Which is your favourite exchange between any two characters at the Netherfield ball (Chapter 18), and why?
- What does it show about Elizabeth that she turns down Mr Collins?

take a break now: it's time to prepare for a journey to Kent

Chapters 22–29, *To Kent*

- Elizabeth is aghast when Charlotte accepts Collins in marriage.
- Jane is cast down by news that Mr Bingley has left the neighbourhood.
- She goes to stay with the Gardiners, her aunt and uncle in London.
- Elizabeth drops in to see her on her way to visit Charlotte in Kent.

Charlotte isn't fooling herself when she accepts Collins's offer. She is only, after all, practising the fatalistic philosophy she has preached (Chapter 6, pp. 69–70). *I am not romantic you know*, she tells Elizabeth. But can Charlotte really afford to be? What real choice does she have? What real choice, ultimately, will Elizabeth herself have? While it may offend our sense of readerly propriety that Collins should even dream of approaching Elizabeth, the reality is that she has no reason to set her sights any higher than Charlotte's. We don't seriously expect her to lose out in the end, but we should see how badly the odds are stacking up against her. Jane's alternative view of the Collins–Charlotte match (Chapter 24, p. 174) is a necessary counter to Elizabeth's idealism. The sisters' conversation here represents a mini-debate on the whole question of love and integrity in marriage.

DISAPPOINTMENT AND DISCONTENT

Disillusioned with her friend Charlotte, and disappointed on Jane's behalf over Bingley's departure, Elizabeth seems, too, in the grip of a greater discontent. *The more I see of the world*, she tells Jane (Chapter 24, pp. 173–4), *the more am I dissatisfied with it; and every day confirms my belief of the inconsistency of all human characters, and of the little dependence that can be placed on the appearance of either merit or sense.* Elizabeth has of course only very recently begun to see anything much of the world at all. Since the action of the novel opened (in early November), her rather narrow world has expanded, but at the same time become less cosy. She has seen things to disappoint her. The very fact that she *can* take new things on board and adjust her view of things is cause for hope, however. That is how people grow.

Longbourn life seems to be emptying out now – Bingley and his party having gone, and Charlotte soon to be leaving with her new husband. The field has been left to Wickham, and his view of things is now taken as the truth. *Every body was pleased to think how much they had always disliked Mr Darcy before they had known any thing of the matter* – not so much Pride and Prejudice as Pride *in* Prejudice! Elizabeth's aunt Mrs Gardiner, too, is taken in by Wickham's pleasing manner, but she remains detached enough to warn her niece not to get too involved. There is no matrimonial mileage in it, she points out (Chapter 26, p. 181). Mrs Gardiner is, in a sense, stepping into the gap left by Charlotte as Elizabeth's older confidante. Coming originally from Derbyshire, and being down at the moment from her home in London, she represents a bigger, broader world than Elizabeth has previously inhabited.

 As we have seen, Charlotte's marriage gives Jane Austen an opportunity to raise the question of compromise in love, and to display, by implication, her heroine's feelings about love and marriage. It has less immediate consequences too, however. Reducing the intelligent companionship available to Elizabeth at home, it adds a little more to her sense of dissatisfaction at Longbourn. But it also opens up another world – another place for her to go and stay. The fact that the friendship, though altered by what has happened, still survives the shock of Charlotte's marriage is touching testimony to Elizabeth's loyalty. But it also points to her capacity to adjust to new circumstances, to grow.

LETTERS FROM LONDON

Jane's letters from London in Chapter 26 are among a number of significant letters in *Pride and Prejudice*. Packed with concentrated background information or character clues, these letters also serve the purpose of pushing the plot forward. After reading Jane's letters, Elizabeth and the reader share some privileged information the other characters don't have access to. We are brought a little closer together with Elizabeth, while she is separated a little further from the other characters.

Reading letters is, of course, like reading people: the character in the novel is placed in a position rather like that of the novel's reader. This heightens our identification with Elizabeth at human level, but it also presents the wider problem of how we are to interpret the people around us, their appearance, actions, words. Each character in *Pride and Prejudice* is like a text which has to be read: how should we read Wickham's bold amiability, for example? Though he has charmed everybody with his *general unreserve* (Chapter 24, p. 176), how open is he really? Might there be another possible interpretation of his behaviour to be read 'between the lines'? And does Darcy's reserve really stem from an objectionable haughtiness? And what about Jane, and her beautiful but inexpressive quietness: we have Elizabeth to interpret her meanings for us, but how are others to read her?

WICKHAM AT WORK

Wickham, in fact, is already coming across as a more complicated character. He is now, it seems, r*endering himself agreeable* (the phrase suggests the conscious way in which he works on his self-presentation) to Mary King, a young lady whose *most remarkable charm* is her ten thousand pounds (Chapter 26, p. 186). Elizabeth's ready acceptance of this convinces her that, whatever she may have been feeling for Wickham, it cannot have been love. But there is of course a glaring double standard in her easy tolerance towards Wickham (*handsome men must have something to live on*) and her crushing disapproval of Charlotte's compromise. This discrepancy will be underlined even more strongly when Elizabeth talks the matter over with Mrs Gardiner (Chapter 27, pp. 188–9).

GOING PLACES

The trip to Kent offers Elizabeth a change of scene. How much she needs that is captured beautifully in Jane Austen's description of the first stage of the journey, to London: *Sir William Lucas, and his daughter Maria, a good humoured girl, but as empty-headed as himself, had nothing to say that could be worth hearing, and were listened to with about as much delight as the rattle of the chaise. Elizabeth loved absurdities, but she had known Sir William's too long. He could tell her nothing new ... and his civilities were worn out like his information.* Elizabeth's love of the absurd is something she has in common with her father. She, however, is outgrowing Longbourn, as her father has not been able to.

What Elizabeth needs is some new experiences – fresh input for a life grown stale. *You give me fresh life and vigour,* she says when Mrs Gardiner raises the idea of a visit to the Lakes: *Adieu to disappointment and spleen. What are men to rocks and mountains?* The sarcasm in the question is obvious and entertaining, but there is something more profound here too: a sense of Elizabeth's capacity to find personal renewal in the natural world. (It was in the Lake District, of course, that the Romantic Wordsworth had written his poetry, and developed his theory that humanity's truest inspiration was to be found in nature.) We can't imagine Mrs Bennet or Lydia in such a setting: Elizabeth, however, has the imagination to appreciate a big, beautiful landscape. Offering her, quite literally, broader horizons, the idea of a Lakeland trip confirms our sense that Elizabeth is somehow bigger, better, than her present circumstances.

ELIZABETH ON THE MOVE

Travel is not just a geographical progression from place to place. It means something internal, spiritual and emotional. Even when he was travelling to London, we saw earlier in this chapter, Sir William Lucas remained stuck in the same old loop of worn-out anecdotes. But the very *thought* of her summer journey is sufficient to liberate Elizabeth to think of new possibilities. She has the capacity to be nourished, modified by new scenes and beautiful landscapes:

> *Oh! What hours of transport we shall spend! And when we do return, it shall not be like other travellers, without being able to give one accurate idea of any thing. We will know where we have gone – we will recollect what we have seen.*

Elizabeth is not prepared, as Sir William is, to travel without actually going anywhere. She is looking to bring something back from her journey, to allow it to influence her. But it is significant, too, that the recollection and the analysis afterwards seems to be, for her, as important as the trip itself. (You would be well advised to develop a similar attitude in your revision!) Vigorous as she is in her physical life – the walks she loves to take outdoors, for example – Elizabeth's intellectual energy is every bit as strong. That comes through in the rhythm of this speech, whose vehemence is signalled by its emphases. Compare it, for example, with Jane Austen's beautifully understated picture of tedium and boredom at the chapter's opening, above (p. 187): *sometimes dirty and sometimes cold, did January and February pass away.* This is the full extent of the variety: from *dirty* to *cold*!

While Lady Catherine may intimidate the others, *Elizabeth's courage did not fail her. She had heard nothing of Lady Catherine that spoke her awful from any extraordinary talents or miraculous virtue, and the mere stateliness of money and rank, she thought she could witness without trepidation* (Chapter 29, p. 196).

Elizabeth's refusal to be cowed by Lady Catherine's bullying reminds us how independent-minded she is. She is surprised that Lady Catherine doesn't find Collins's flattery tiresome. She

COMMENTARY

shouldn't be, of course: Lady Catherine may get a sense of power from impressing her guests with new and exotic dishes (p. 197), but she herself is just dining off praise. She has her guests where she wants them, telling her what she wants to hear. For all the chatter of admiration, we are told, *the party did not supply much conversation* (pp. 197–8), while at the after-dinner card game *their table was superlatively stupid. Scarcely a syllable was uttered*. Grand it may be, but this is a sterile scene, its only animation being in Jane Austen's amusing account of the situation and of Elizabeth's spirited refusal to be overawed. These characters are not going anywhere; certainly, nothing in their lives is going to match Elizabeth's development.

Having said which, the grotesque impertinence of Lady Catherine's questioning should not blind us to the fact that it reveals some very useful information for us as readers. Elizabeth's unconventional education (Chapter 29, p. 199) explains her own originality as a character. At the same time, however, its casual nature helps to explain the silliness of her younger sisters: *such of us as wished to learn, never wanted the means ... Those who chose to be idle, certainly might.*

Your turn

? Why is Elizabeth upset when Charlotte accepts Mr Collins (Chapter 22)?

? What is the significance of Miss Bingley's letter to Jane (Chapter 24)?

? What in Wickham's behaviour shows us that he is unlikely to be in love with Elizabeth? Are we given any clues as to how strong her feelings may have been? Draw a Mini Mind Map to help you.

? In your own words, describe Rosings and how life there differs from life at Longbourn.

you're about to meet an old friend, but first take a break

Chapters 30–3: *Re-enter Mr Darcy*

- Mr Darcy arrives at Rosings, come to visit his aunt, Lady Catherine.
- Praising his cousin, Fitzwilliam tells Elizabeth how Darcy saved his friend Bingley from a 'most imprudent marriage'.

HER OWN WOMAN

In the meantime, though, Elizabeth enjoys herself most in her own company. (✪ Do you?) Again, her love of the outdoors reminds us not only of her physical vigour but of her richness in inner resources and her ability to find inspiration in Nature. *Her favourite walk ... we find* (Chapter 30, p. 203), *was along the open grove which edged that side of the park, where there was a nice sheltered path, which no one seemed to value but herself, and where she felt beyond the reach of Lady Catherine's curiosity.* Words such as *open* and *sheltered* here suggest that the landscape welcomes and protects her, while her originality and capacity to see deeper than others is underlined by her having found a path which *no one seemed to value but herself.* (✪ Can you think of anything in your own life that corresponds to this?)

Mr Darcy, when Elizabeth meets him again, shows *his usual reserve* (Chapter 30, p. 204). The good news, as he smoulders silently away during the ladies' conversation with Fitzwilliam, is that he hasn't changed. His feelings for Elizabeth, we sense as readers, remain strong as ever, even if she has no inkling of them. But the bad news, too, is that he hasn't changed – has not adjusted, grown, as he needs to.

Being *about thirty, not handsome, but in person and address most truly the gentleman*, Fitzwilliam's manner offsets his lack of good looks. *He entered into conversation directly with the readiness and ease of a well-bred man*, while Darcy maintains his stony silence. (Jane Austen will of course pick up this idea in the next chapter, in the wonderful sparring scene between Darcy and Elizabeth at the piano.)

COMMENTARY

LADY CATHERINE PERFORMS

This episode is set up beautifully, with Lady Catherine's absurdly arrogant account of her own musical taste. *It is of all subjects my delight,* she says (Chapter 31, p. 207). *There are few people who have more true enjoyment* (other people, it seems, have only false enjoyment!) *of music than myself, or a better natural taste.* It comes as a shock after such self-praise to find that neither she nor her daughter even plays any instrument: *If I had ever learnt, I should have been a great proficient. And so would Anne, if her health had allowed her to apply.* It's hilarious, of course, but there is a more serious point too. Lady Catherine talks about accomplishment, but doesn't actually have any. She talks a lot about gentility; her nephew Darcy, however, is embarrassed by her *ill-breeding* (p. 207).

So great is Lady Catherine's love of music that she talks over Elizabeth's playing. Darcy hints at his own independence from her authority (and thus, of course, his kinship with Lady Catherine's only other resister, Elizabeth herself) by moving away from his aunt *And moving with his usual deliberation towards the piano forte, stationed himself so as to command a full view of the fair performer's countenance.*

> The phrase *his usual deliberation* here, like *his usual reserve* above (Chapter 30, p. 204) hints at Darcy's reliability.

SPARRING PARTNERS

You mean to frighten me ... charges Elizabeth (Chapter 31, p. 208). He answers her as elegantly as she challenges him: reserved as he is, Darcy always finds the wit to tease Elizabeth back when she teases him. This is one way in which Elizabeth's prejudice has blinded her to his true worth: Darcy has much more sense of humour than she gives him credit for. Having laughed at herself, Elizabeth teasingly threatens shocking revelations about him. Light-hearted as it is, his response – *I am not afraid of you* – is also a statement of trust in her goodwill, and a claim too that he knows her well enough to have no fears. Once again, Elizabeth is oblivious to something the reader senses unmistakably here. There is real animation, real sparkle in this conversation, and for all its light jokiness, real intimacy.

If Darcy claims to have got Elizabeth's measure, she hints that she knows him too. *Shall we ask him why a man of sense and education, and who has lived in the world, is ill qualified to recommend himself to strangers?* Her mocking question actually gets right to the heart of Darcy's problem as a character, while her scornful reaction to his claim that he doesn't have the *talent* of making small talk and socialising exposes the laziness involved in his position. Darcy's smile when she scores these hits suggests surprising tenderness on the part of such an austere, unyielding man, while his comment that *We neither of us perform to strangers* hints at closeness and kinship.

THE MORNING AFTER

Next morning, it is as if none of this ever happened. While they spark off one another in company, once left alone together Elizabeth and Darcy are like strangers – and of course neither of them *perform to strangers*. Their conversation, once they manage to get a conversation of sorts going, is creaky and faltering. It is not without significance, though. Their little disagreement over what constitutes a long distance (Chapter 32, p. 212) is one example of this. Not only does it point to the fact that men of their class move in a much larger world than home-bound women do, but it also prepares the way for a more personal understanding. Darcy is touched by her love of home – and, perhaps, by her closeness and loyalty to those she loves. He admires the responsibility she feels towards her family, even as he is aware that her family is her liability. (The great service he will do her for love, of course, will be to take that responsibility upon himself over Lydia's elopement.) We see how Elizabeth continues to misunderstand him too, however. When (Chapter 32, p. 212) she *sees a smile she fancied she understood*, it is clear that she has misread his meaning entirely. But then Darcy's feelings towards Elizabeth at this time are generally difficult to read: Charlotte, we learn a few pages later (p. 215), *as she liked to believe this change* [in Darcy's behaviour] *the effect of love, and the object of that love, her friend Eliza, she sat herself seriously to work to find it out. – She watched him whenever they were at Rosings, and whenever he came to Hunsford; but without much success.*

COMMENTARY

🌳 Darcy senses, as we have done, that Elizabeth has outgrown her life in Longbourn. She seems to him to belong to a far wider world. *You cannot have a right to such very strong local attachment. You cannot have been always at Longbourn,* he tells her (p. 213). Then, as if he has shown too much of his true feelings, he promptly backs off, picks up a newspaper and asks politely how she likes Kent. Having for a moment taken on the more personal, spiritual sense we talked about in Chapter 27, travel has suddenly slipped back into the more everyday sense of moving from place to place, and whether Kent is as nice as Hertfordshire!

Jane Austen has great fun with Elizabeth and Darcy during this section of the novel. Both seem out of their depth. Darcy keeps calling at the Parsonage, only to sit in silence. Meanwhile, for all her normal sharpness, Elizabeth is both baffled and exasperated by her 'unexpected' meetings with Darcy. *She felt all the perverseness of the mischance that should bring him where no one else was brought.* Yet if her attempts to avoid him founder in farce, there is the more serious implication here, too, that he can reach her, emotionally, where others cannot. Elizabeth's confusion about Darcy's motives must stem in part from their difference in social rank. Too modest and straight to be ambitious or calculating, she really cannot imagine why he would be interested in her. Her slowness on the uptake and flustered irritation also suggest a degree of sexual confusion. Darcy stirs feelings in her that she is too inexperienced to recognise, let alone understand. She is growing up as a woman, and doesn't yet realise it. For such a bright girl, Elizabeth is really quite dim where Darcy is concerned. His hints that she might be staying at Rosings in future (Chapter 33, p. 215) surely suggest the possibility of her visiting as his wife. To her, however, they make no sense whatsoever.

If Elizabeth's meetings with Darcy have not been as coincidental as she has thought, the coincidence that she has just been *re-perusing Jane's last letter* when she learns from Colonel Fitzwilliam about Darcy's part in heading off Bingley's relationship with Jane is real enough. Her shock must of course only be increased by her realisation that whatever goes for Jane goes for her. Any hopes she may have of Darcy at the moment must obviously be subconscious – her conscious indifference towards him is clear, and clearly genuine. It must still be shocking to think, however, that if it would be *most imprudent* for a man of Bingley's rank to link himself with Jane, what would it be for Darcy, his obvious social superior, to be associated with Elizabeth? The emotional blow that Jane's loss (and her own potential one) causes her, manifesting itself physically in *agitation and tears* and *headache* (Chapter 33, p. 219), ironically serves the purpose in the plot of keeping Elizabeth home alone when the others go out, giving Darcy the opportunity he needs to come and see her.

What do you think?

? In Chapter 31, find three comments of Mr Darcy which show his admiration for Elizabeth.
? Which of Elizabeth's occupations particularly come to the fore during her stay in Kent?

take some time off now: you'll need to be fully psyched up for Mr Darcy's proposal!

Chapters 34–7, *Another proposal!*

- Darcy proposes to the astonished Elizabeth.
- She refuses contemptuously: he's destroyed her sister's happiness, she says, not to mention blighting Wickham's prospects.
- Next day, Darcy hands her a letter defending his actions.

There have been a number of coincidences real and imagined during Elizabeth's time in Kent. Darcy is not, of course, to blame for being the second man to have proposed to Elizabeth in recent weeks, but he is at fault for being the second to make his proposal insulting. A proposal of marriage is supposed to be a compliment, but Darcy's (Chapter 34, p. 221) isn't, any more than in its way than Collins's was (Chapter 20). Darcy discourses upon the inferiority of her connections, the struggle he has put up to resist her. Elizabeth's feelings that she should

COMMENTARY

be courteous are ultimately overcome by his protests of how unwelcome to him his feelings have been and, most of all, by the fact that: *He spoke of apprehension and anxiety, but his countenance expressed real security.* Darcy resembles Collins in his inability to imagine the possibility of refusal.

DARCY GETS A SHOCK

Elizabeth's charge that he has behaved in an ungentlemanlike manner hits home forcibly enough to make Darcy *start* (Chapter 34, p. 224). As readers we wonder whether the shock Elizabeth's refusal has caused him will mire him in resentment or jolt him into change. Indignant as she is, meanwhile, Elizabeth feels conscious after he leaves that his love for her has been strong enough to overcome *all the objections which had made him prevent his friend's marrying her sister, and which must appear at least with equal force in his own case* (Chapter 35, p. 224). Whatever her personal dislike for Mr Darcy, his declaration of love has in some strange way, we sense, extended her horizons, enlarged her possibilities as a person.

Out walking next day, she has another of her unexpected meetings with Darcy (see Chapter 33), only this time there's no pretence of coincidence. *I have been walking in the grove some time in the hope of meeting you,* he admits. Then he retreats, and lets his letter speak for him. Having failed so completely to get through to her in person, perhaps he will do better in writing? As we have already seen, letters play an important role in *Pride and Prejudice.* This one gets across a considerable amount of background information (revelations about Wickham, Georgiana, and, of course, Darcy's own character and attitudes) in a short space of time. It also gives Jane Austen an opportunity to track back through the story so far, giving us a different perspective on a tale that's been told very much from Elizabeth's point of view.

His interpretation of events is of course very different from hers. Using words suggestive of close study (*observed, perceive … scrutiny,* Chapter 35, p. 228), Darcy describes watching Bingley and Jane in the attempt to read their feelings. Though his friend, he admits, seemed more smitten than he had ever known him, Jane did not appear to feel as strongly. Darcy admits in the first part of his letter that he may have been wrong about Jane. This is balanced in the second part by his invitation to Elizabeth to consider whether she herself might not have been mistaken in her view of Wickham, who appears in a very different light in Darcy's account. Though Wickham has of course aired his side of the story repeatedly and at length, we have not heard Darcy's side of things before. The story of his attempted elopement with Georgiana Darcy, while revealing a new and much less likeable aspect of Wickham's character, reveals something about Darcy too. We have seen how private a person he is – he admits this is one reason for his not having exposed Wickham at the time. Yet he is revealing it now – a considerable act of trust in the woman who only the day before contemptuously rejected him. *Having said thus much, I feel no doubt of your secrecy*, he says (Chapter 35, p. 231). Having formed his estimation of Elizabeth, he is not going to let the ups and downs of their daily dealings, however unpleasant, alter his view of her fundamental integrity. There is a big-hearted nobility about this that Elizabeth could hardly fail to find impressive.

THE LETTER

Elizabeth of course devours Darcy's letter. Chapter 36 is all but entirely given over to her reading and re-reading. It's an upsetting, tumultuously confusing experience. *Her feelings as she read were scarcely to be defined*, we are told (p. 233), and the stop-start style here reflects this: *She read, with an eagerness which hardly left her power of comprehension, and from an impatience of knowing what the next sentence might bring, was incapable of attending to the sense of the one before her eyes.* This sentence seems to pull up short after its terse opening statement *She read*, before unravelling in two much longer clauses, neither of which brings the main verb (*was incapable*) which gives the sentence the firm direction we feel it needs.

Jane Austen's prose here mirrors the confusion in Elizabeth's mind, the helter-skelter haste with which she is skip-reading, and back-tracking, the struggle she is having to assimilate and assess all she is being told. Elizabeth is having her mind changed, and it is a violent, traumatic experience. She puts the letter away, then takes it out and reads it again, picks out particular sections and tries to match them with her own recollections. Then she tries to re-read Wickham in her memory. *She could see him instantly before her, in every charm of air and address; but she could remember no more substantial good than the general approbation of the neighbourhood, and the regard which his social powers had gained him in the mess.*

Jane Austen's insistence on the vivid exactness of Elizabeth's memories is interesting. She wants us to understand that Elizabeth – and we as readers – are not reading two different stories but re-reading, and reinterpreting, the same text we read before – though this time it does indeed read like a different story. Wickham's now-sinister smoothness is suggested in the even rhythm of a sentence like: *His countenance, voice, and manner had established him at once in the possession of every virtue.* Elizabeth ransacks her memory in search of a kind action on his part to lend some sense of reality to his appearance of kindness, *But no such recollection befriended her.*

Of all the acts of reading in *Pride and Prejudice*, this one is the most important, marking a pivotal point in the novel. Darcy's letter takes on for Elizabeth an almost scriptural significance. She has misunderstood Darcy completely, she realises, and been badly mistaken about Wickham. More than that, though, these gross errors indicate her own vanity and folly – she who has prided herself so on her sharpness. The humiliating conclusion she is forced to reach is that *Till this moment, I never knew myself* (Chapter 36, p. 237). What Darcy says about Jane's feelings for Bingley show that he was indeed mistaken. But the mistake is understandable; indeed it confirms Charlotte's earlier reservations (Chapter 6, pp. 68–9). Beautiful as it is, Jane's still, inexpressive face has been, Elizabeth sees, too blank, too unreadable for her own good.

Looking again at what Darcy says about her family, she has to acknowledge its justice. Their behaviour at the Netherfield ball embarrassed her, but then she has long been accustomed to that. What she is suddenly beginning to sense, however, is that their behaviour to a large extent *defines* her and Jane: whatever qualities she and Jane may have, they are followed round by the follies of their mother and sisters, their father's heedlessness. The realisation comes to her now like a bolt from the blue, leaving a character we have come to love for her animation and cheerfulness *depressed beyond any thing she had ever known before* (Chapter 36, p. 237). One way and another, Darcy's letter has, in the course of its five or six pages, turned Elizabeth's whole world upside down. It is hardly surprising that, as Chapter 36 comes to its end, *She could think only of her letter.*

Through Chapter 37, too, the letter is never far from Elizabeth's thoughts: *Mr Darcy's letter*, we are told, *she was in a fair way of soon knowing by heart* (p. 241). As she broods on her own errors of judgement and her family's failures of propriety, *the happy spirits which had seldom been depressed before, were now so much affected as to make it almost impossible for her to appear tolerably cheerful.* This section of the novel ends, then, in a distinctly downbeat mood. The youthful enthusiasm and optimism which has made Elizabeth so attractive has received a felling blow; the breezy self-confidence with which we are used to seeing her lay down the law has been punctured. The question is, can Elizabeth survive – even find a way of growing through – this crushing setback? The naive girl is gone for ever: can she come back as a woman?

Test yourself

? Darcy is divided in his feelings for Elizabeth. What does he see as the case for and against? Arrange your answer in two columns, or as a Mind Map.

? Describe how Darcy sees his relationship with his sister (Chapter 35). What else does his letter tell us about his attitude to the Bennet family as a whole?

? What emerges as the real reason for Jane and Bingley's relationship having ended?

time for a break, before the journey home to Longbourn

COMMENTARY

Chapters 38–42, *Longbourn*

- Longbourn doesn't feel the same any more, peaceful as it is with Lydia gone.
- Elizabeth can't wait to be off on her tour with the Gardiners.
- She's disappointed that time doesn't allow a tour of the Lake District, though, and a bit nervous at the thought of visiting Darcy's county, Derbyshire.

Chapters 39–41 are transitional, showing Elizabeth turning round between her Kent and Derbyshire trips. They also give us a chance to collect our thoughts. Like Elizabeth, we have to give the shock revelations that ended the previous section a chance to sink in. Like Elizabeth, we begin by reconsidering – and radically reassessing – the life of the Bennet family.

When Lydia and Kitty meet her and Jane at the inn, it's as if Elizabeth were seeing them for the first time. As at the moment in Chapter 36, p. 237 when she realised that *Till this moment, I never knew myself*, she feels that in some ways she is seeing herself for the first time too. Lydia's comments on Mary King (Chapter 39, p. 247) are expressed with more coarseness than Elizabeth herself would ever have been guilty of. Cruel and crass as they are, though, they reflect what would have been her own feelings in the past. Lydia's mindless twitterings in the carriage (Chapter 39, pp. 248–9) are beautifully captured by Jane Austen. Lydia's speech is as full of exclamation marks as it is empty of anything approaching sense. She asks questions without waiting for any reply, and slips from subject to subject with dizzying speed and bewildering illogicality. Lydia's frivolous spirit seems to dominate this homecoming, as if in Jane and Elizabeth's absence she has taken over a family on which her older sisters formerly imposed at least some semblance of order and propriety.

The household is full of the Brighton scheme, and though Mr Bennet is in theory refusing his permission, in practice he is not doing so firmly enough to end the excitement (Chapter 39, pp. 249–50). Elizabeth will attempt to persuade him of the need for firmness when Lydia receives her separate invitation to go to Brighton (Chapter 41, p. 258), but he is unwilling – or unable – to take her seriously.

A TALE OF TWO SISTERS

The contrast between Lydia's discourse and Mary's when they get home (*Oh! Mary ... I should infinitely prefer a book*, Chapter 39, p. 249) is comic: again, Lydia's speech is breathless, exclamatory prattle while Mary's grave reply sounds like something from a particularly solemn book, full of pompous phrases like *Far be it from me ... to depreciate such pleasures. They would doubtless be congenial with the generality of female minds*. Jane Austen is making a more serious point here too, however: education is not just about learning by heart but about understanding; learning is no use if it doesn't bring a deeper human insight (worth bearing in mind as you revise for your exams). Mary's mind is every bit as superficial as Lydia's. The one all seriousness, the other all frivolity, these two girls are equally silly.

Lydia's inability to listen (*She seldom listened to any body for more than half a minute*, Chapter 39, p. 249) is of course one reason why she can neither learn nor develop. Mary has much the same problem: she can memorise impressive quotations, but never seems to take on any of their wisdom. Her moral puritanism is untempered by any intellectual understanding or human compassion (think of her absurdly inappropriate sermonising after Lydia's disgrace, Chapter 47, p. 305, for instance); her ladylike accomplishment (her piano playing) is untempered by any social sensitivity (which would, for example, have meant her knowing when to stop, at the Netherfield ball, Chapter 18, p. 142).

Elizabeth gives Jane a version of what Darcy's letter contained, this one of course drastically edited, to include the Wickham material and exclude the bits about Jane and Bingley. Concealment is now an issue between the sisters as it never has been before. Secrets *weighed upon her*, we are told (Chapter 40, p. 253) and yet, open as she is by nature, Elizabeth's world is more complicated now and she cannot confide all she feels. Jane never could, of course, and now all her strength is going into hiding her pain.

COMMENTARY

THE REAL WICKHAM

Seeing Wickham for what she assumes is to be the last time (Chapter 41, p. 259), Elizabeth now perceives him very differently. What used to be his attractions now seem objectionable. (*She had even learnt to detect, in the very gentleness which had first delighted her, an affectation and a sameness to disgust and weary.*) As she taunts him with her new-found knowledge, Wickham is caught offguard. He is *surprised, displeased, alarmed* (p. 260) when Colonel Fitzwilliam's name is mentioned, but collects himself. There is a suggestion of acting in Wickham's behaviour throughout this scene – *an air of indifference ... checking himself ... shaking off his embarrassment ...* – a sense that he is consciously working at his own self-presentation.

A HUSBAND AND WIFE, A FATHER AND DAUGHTER

Chapter 42 opens with a sketch of what her parents' marriage might have taught Elizabeth about marriage in general.

Mr Bennet was, we learn (p. 262), *captivated* by Mrs Bennet's *youth and beauty*. Youth is temporary by definition, of course; beauty, if it is of that superficial physical sort which is, as the proverb says, only 'skin deep', is no more lasting. It is not surprising, then, that in a very short time his *Respect, esteem, and confidence, had vanished for ever*. This analysis is of course one-sided. There is nothing here about what Mrs Bennet might feel, even though, silly as she may be, she is surely not without feelings of her own. This is because Elizabeth, despite seeing Mr Bennet's shortcomings as a husband and father, still identifies strongly with him. *Respecting his abilities, and grateful for his affectionate treatment of herself, she endeavoured to forget what she could not overlook.* There are obvious similarities between father and daughter. *He was fond of the country and of books*, we are told, and so, we know, is Elizabeth. There is a crucial difference, though. For her, both reading and walking are ways of getting out into the world, out of herself, of growing. Her father lives in the country because he can't be bothered with society; his library, far from being a window on the world, is a refuge from it.

59

PRIDE AND PREJUDICE

📖 On the face of it, the obvious place for such background material would have been at the beginning of the novel. Instead, Jane Austen has allowed us to share Elizabeth's partial view of things. Like her, we have been aware of Mr Bennet's irresponsibility, but have liked him too much to appreciate its full seriousness. Elizabeth could not have been so lively a character as she is had she realised when she was younger quite how depressing her family circumstances really were. Darcy's letter has sobered her up all of a sudden – and us with her. Like her, we have the sensation of looking back and seeing that what seemed like harmless humour was something far more damaging.

Excited at the thought of her holiday with the Gardiners, Elizabeth can't even see the word 'Derbyshire' without thinking of Darcy's house at Pemberley and of Darcy himself. She is able to laugh at her preoccupation, though, a sign that her spirits are partly restored. The prospect of travel is itself restorative. Wherever it takes her, whatever she finds, it will represent an escape from the surroundings at Longbourn she is now finding increasingly cramped. *One enjoyment was certain* she considers – *that of suitableness as companions.*

🐞 She doesn't say it – doesn't need to – but she can no longer regard her own immediate family in that way.

Meanwhile, Jane Austen is having fun with Elizabeth's anxieties. Derbyshire is a big place, and it's obviously silly for Elizabeth to assume that she is inevitably going to run into Darcy. As she herself sees in her more rational moments: *But surely ... I may enter his county with impunity* (Chapter 42, p. 265). Within a page or so, however, cheekily shrugging off any duty to describe the ins and outs of their journey north, Jane Austen has delivered her travellers to Lambton – where, conveniently enough, Mrs Gardiner once lived – and to the very threshold of Pemberley!

What do you think?

?   Does Elizabeth come back to a happy home at Longbourn? What clues can you find in the text?

COMMENTARY

? What are Elizabeth's reasons for not telling everybody in the neighbourhood what she knows about Wickham (Chapter 40)?

? What reason does Mr Bennet give for letting Lydia go to Brighton after all (Chapter 41)?

? Look at the conversation between Elizabeth and Wickham in Chapter 41. What words and phrases suggest Wickham's discomfort in this scene? What attempts does he make to hide it?

an unexpected encounter — after the break

Chapter 43–6, *Derbyshire*

◆ Elizabeth is impressed by Pemberley, but even more impressed by the change in its owner's manner towards her.
◆ She is shocked at the news that Lydia has run away with Wickham.

Pemberley and its grounds don't just belong to Darcy – in some sense they represent him. And, consequently, what Elizabeth might herself have been, had she accepted him (*And of this place ... I might have been mistress!*, Chapter 43, p. 269). Elizabeth can read in the house and grounds things she has never understood before about the man.

At the most obvious level, of course, Pemberley proclaims Darcy's wealth and rank. To Elizabeth, however (and to us if we're prepared to read the scene carefully) it says much more.

The park was very large, we find (Chapter 43, p. 267), *and contained great variety of ground.* Darcy too, it strikes us, may contain more variety than Elizabeth has yet appreciated. Of solid *stone*, the *handsome* house, which Jane Austen describes as *standing well* in its setting, gives an impression of its owner's steadiness and reliability, his unshowy good looks. There is no *artificial appearance* in the scene, we are assured, the banks of the stream being *neither formal, nor falsely adorned.* There is no deception here, no pretence at anything that isn't really true. The sheer scale and spaciousness of the house and park, meanwhile, contrast very obviously with the cramped, constricting surroundings with which Elizabeth is familiar. Longbourn's little garden is nothing to this open, liberating landscape.

Within the house, too, we find testimony to the absent owner's character. The housekeeper's devoted description (Chapter 43, pp. 269–71) shows us a new and different Darcy: a loving brother, a considerate employer, a generous landlord. And if the housekeeper contradicts Elizabeth's opinion as to Darcy's temper, it is this gentler character which Elizabeth will find confirmed when she studies (as we are told she does for *several minutes ... in earnest contemplation*, Chapter 43, p. 271) his sister's smiling portrait of him. It is a smile she has seen before, she realises, but it has taken Georgiana's picture to enable her properly to see it, just as it has taken the sight of his home to enable her to appreciate other aspects of his character.

MR DARCY IN PERSON

After the house and the picture, there's an unexpected opportunity to study the man himself. The first meeting between the two catches both offguard. We can read it in their body language: their blushes, and the fact that *He absolutely started, and for a moment seemed immoveable from surprise*, whilst *she had instinctively turned away* (Chapter 43, p. 272). Even when she recovers enough to talk to him, Elizabeth can hardly look him in the eye. She is *Amazed at the alteration in his manner since they last parted.* Now, a man she has always thought arrogant seems diffident and vulnerable. Despite his shock, his friendliness seems completely unforced.

If there is an *alteration in his manner*, it suggests that there has been an alteration in his character. Darcy, it seems, has been changed by her rejection of the previous year, and grown in humility. Yet the alteration isn't only in him, of course. Elizabeth views him differently now because she too has learned from her experiences. Just as earlier (Chapter 41, p. 259) we saw that Wickham's most winning features now seem to her the most obvious clues to his worthlessness, so Darcy's reserve and social stiffness now seem interpretable as signs of quiet integrity and reliability.

COMMENTARY

There is another thing about this encounter which makes it easier than many of their earlier meetings. For the first time, Elizabeth is not being let down by her family. She appears to best advantage with the Gardiners, who are far more fitting parent-figures than her actual mother and father. Elizabeth cannot help being moved by the fact that Darcy wants her to meet *his* surviving family in the shape of his sister (p. 277), especially given that he told her the secret of Georgiana's past in his letter (Chapter 35, p. 231). The trust he felt in Elizabeth then he still feels, it is clear. The way he asks her too – humbly, as if she, Elizabeth, will be doing him a great favour – suggests that his tenderness for her remains the same, but that he has lost the bumptious sense of entitlement which made his proposal (Chapter 34) so insulting. Meeting Georgiana next morning at the inn (Chapter 44), Elizabeth is struck by the *sense and good humour* in her face (p. 281). Her gentle, unassuming manner contrasts with that of the severe-seeming Darcy, but it does him credit, too, since it was he who brought her up.

THE BINGLEY QUICKSTEP

Bingley's quick step on the stair (Chapter 44, p. 281) restores the Bingley–Jane romantic plot, shelved much earlier, to the foreground. The sound suggests his eagerness to meet Elizabeth but *quick* suggests too his spontaneity, his readiness, recalling in addition the conversation about his impetuousness at Netherfield (Chapter 10, pp. 93–4). You don't even need to see him, then, to realise that he hasn't changed – an impression which is confirmed by the *unaffected cordiality* of his manner once he actually comes into the room. This is reassuring, of course; if Bingley is the same in these other respects, it seems likely that he will be feeling the same way about Jane.

The Gardiners, meanwhile, can't believe what is happening. They are *all amazement* (Chapter 44, p. 280) that someone so grand as Darcy should be calling on them at all. At Hunsford (Chapter 32, p. 215), Charlotte watched events and wondered what was going on, setting *herself seriously to work* studying Darcy's face to try to work out the meaning of his behaviour. This time it is the Gardiners who are placed in the position of readers trying to understand the narrative unfolding before them. Their position within the novel is rather like ours outside it. They are witnessing this scene at first hand, though, so it is interesting to find their impressions tallying with our own: *Of the lady's sensations they remained a little in doubt; but that the gentleman was overflowing with admiration was evident enough* (Chapter 44, p. 281). Mrs Gardiner attempts to read Elizabeth's reaction to Darcy's invitation to Pemberley the next day, but finds that her niece has turned away her head. The gesture excludes us too: Elizabeth's feelings at this point are too private to be shared, even with Jane Austen's reader. Their reading of Darcy finds in him something very different from what they have heard about, *and had they drawn his character from their own feelings, and his servant's report, without any reference to any other account, the circle in Hertfordshire to which he was known, would not have recognised it for Mr Darcy* (Chapter 44, p. 284).

A SLEEPLESS NIGHT

If Mrs Gardiner cannot read Elizabeth's feelings, neither can Elizabeth herself. She lies awake *two whole hours* that night *endeavouring to make them out* (Chapter 44, p. 284). She feels respect and esteem, we are told, but chiefly *gratitude* for his continuing to be so warm towards her after the way she has behaved to him. Emotionally, of course, Elizabeth is in a turmoil. *She respected, she esteemed...* (p. 285): with its rolling list of feelings, this sentence seems to run away with itself, rather as Elizabeth's feelings are doing with her.

A BEAUTIFUL SETTING

Jane Austen sets the scene for the next day's visit to Pemberley with some care. Elizabeth and the Gardiners are shown into a saloon whose open, full-length windows make the wooded parkland and walls outside as much a part of the backdrop as the room itself. This is one of the few occasions in *Pride and Prejudice* where we find such a visually appealing, sensuous scene. It's a welcoming setting for Elizabeth, who has often shown herself to be more at ease outdoors (see, for instance, Chapter 7, p. 79, Chapter 27, p. 187, Chapter 30, p. 203).

Inside (Chapter 45, p. 287), we find not just a beautiful, airy room but a lavish display of exotic food (*beautiful pyramids of grapes, nectarines, and peaches*). It's as if everything – from the *oaks and Spanish chesnuts* outside to the fruit bowls within – has been laid on for Elizabeth's benefit.

The grace and nobility of this scene is too complete to be destroyed by Mrs Hurst and Miss Bingley's snobbishness, even though the chill they exude may kill conversation. Their pride is different from Darcy's: it really is about rank and wealth pure and simple. Miss Bingley sits in stony silence for *a quarter of an hour* before managing a *cold enquiry* about Elizabeth's family (Chapter 45, p. 287). In attempting to engage the visitors in conversation, Mrs Annesley reveals herself as being *more truly well-bred than either of the others*: Mrs Annesley, *genteel and agreeable-looking*, seems to fit in harmoniously here, but Caroline Bingley's sneering voice is discordant. The grace of these surroundings is against Miss Bingley: her *ill-natured attack* (p. 288) stands no chance of success – only reducing her standing still further, indeed, when the jibe she aims at Elizabeth about the militia misses its target altogether, catching her supposed friend Georgiana instead. Elizabeth's refusal to rise to the provocation allows Georgiana to compose herself quietly, leaving Elizabeth the undisputed victor in this unacknowledged contest.

A FAMILY AFFAIR

Yet in Elizabeth's hour of triumph, her family comes back to haunt her. If things have been hotting up here in Derbyshire, further south, in Brighton, Lydia has been busy too.

Jane's two letters (one would have done had Jane Austen wanted just to get across the bald facts of the case) build suspense, giving us a sense of the mounting seriousness of a still-developing situation. Jane is writing to the moment, we feel, as events unfold. Elizabeth practically collapses on receiving the news: this is a disaster not only for her family but for her personally. It is ironic that Darcy was very likely coming to propose to her a second time. Instead, he finds himself mopping up a helpless and utterly vulnerable girl. Elizabeth is *unable to support herself*; it is *impossible for him to leave her*.

The occasion shows us Darcy's kinder, softer side. By the time she is sufficiently composed to start thinking about Darcy, however, Elizabeth is seeing his gloomy, abstracted manner as he hears her story, his pacing as he considers what she is saying (Chapter 46, p. 295), and drawing quite different conclusions.

To her, his manner suggests her *sinking power* now that her family's disgrace is complete. She is, however, misreading him. This whole central section of the novel has foregrounded Elizabeth and her life, allowing us to consider her outside the context of her family, first in Kent and now in Derbyshire. Now it seems this has been no more than an interlude, as her family forces its way violently back into the picture. *Self, though it would intrude, could not engross her* (Chapter 46, p. 295): Elizabeth's own happiness will have to be set aside now. Whatever her own individual merits, she is defined by her family, she feels. Dream as she may, she will always be her mother's daughter, sister not only of Jane but of Lydia, Kitty and Mary.

Any thoughts?

- ? What delights Elizabeth especially about the park at Pemberley (Chapter 43)?
- ? The Gardiners are *all amazement* at Darcy's visit to the inn (Chapter 44). Why?
- ? What changes do we see in Elizabeth to suggest that she's started to feel differently about Darcy? Look not only at Jane Austen's discussion of her feelings but her gestures and physical symptoms.
- ? News of Lydia's elopement upsets Elizabeth on a number of different levels. Can you think of two reasons for her distress?

take some time off now, to get over the shock of Lydia's elopement: there's a busy final section ahead

COMMENTARY

Chapters 47–61: *Three weddings and a visit from Lady Catherine*

- Mr Gardiner takes over the hunt for the runaways. They're finally found in London, and their marriage arranged.
- At Longbourn with her new husband, Lydia lets slip that Darcy was at their wedding, Elizabeth, appalled, writes to Mrs Gardiner to ask what he was doing there.
- It was Darcy who found the missing couple, her aunt replies, and who paid Wickham to do the decent thing.
- Bingley and Jane become engaged.
- Lady Catherine comes to call, warning Elizabeth to break off her engagement with Darcy. There is no engagement, says the astonished Elizabeth – but she refuses to promise not to enter into any in the future.
- A few days later, indeed, she does just that. Darcy calls and proposes once more. This time she doesn't send him packing.

For all the fuss there has been, Longbourn seems the same only more so when Elizabeth gets home. There is, we feel, a certain logic, an inevitability about what has happened. This is the way it's always been. It's just that, instead of being hidden away in his study, Mr Bennet is absent in London, failing to find his missing daughter; instead of being simply silly, Mrs Bennet is hysterical, and about as much use as if she were a child herself. Described as *deranged* earlier (Chapter 46, p. 49) the family certainly seems to be falling apart now. It is up to Elizabeth and Jane to take care of things – though once again, what is so different about that? Elizabeth finds her mother *blaming every body but the person to whose ill judging indulgence the errors of her daughter must be principally owing* (Chapter 47, p. 303). Ironically, Elizabeth and Jane are far quicker to take responsibility for what has happened, berating themselves in hindsight for not having exposed Wickham (p. 307).

LYDIA'S LETTER

The girlish prattle of Lydia's letter (Chapter 47, p. 307) brings home to us more forcefully than ever the fact that the same text can have different interpretations. *You will laugh*

67

when you know where I am gone, she writes: just how wrong can she be? The gap between the spirit in which this letter was written and spirit in which it will be read is enormous. The other thing this letter brings home to us is Lydia's sheer thoughtlessness – a fault which, as we have seen, Jane Austen considers anything but trivial. Lydia has run away not in a spirit of uncontrollable passion but in a spirit of undisciplined fun. Though she says that *There is but one man in the world I love,* a few lines later she is chatting cheerfully about Pratt and thinking about the next ball, and the slit in her muslin gown — all of which questions seem equally important to her.

A REPENTANT MR BENNET?

Mr Bennet has an intelligence and a self-awareness his wife lacks, but is he really so much more admirable? *No, Lizzy,* he says when she tells him not to be too hard on himself, *let me once in my life feel how much I have been to blame. I am not afraid of being overpowered by the impression. It will pass away soon enough* (Chapter 48, p. 314). His ironic self-deprecation here is almost touching. At the same time, however, he is effectively admitting that he has no intention of changing. His self-knowledge is all too accurate: his sense of guilt really will pass away soon enough. (*When the first transports of rage which had produced his activity in seeking her were over, he naturally returned to all his former indolence,* Chapter 50, p. 323.) His experience will not change him, as Elizabeth's and Darcy's experiences change them. Unlike his wife, he sees the problem, and knows what is required. But he is not prepared to make the necessary exertion. Like Mrs Bennet, then, he is incapable of developing, of growing.

NEWS FROM LONDON

Another letter, another text. What is most interesting in Mr Gardiner's letter, however, is what *is not* in it. It is obvious that some deal has been struck – but what? A text speaks to us not only in its lines but 'between the lines'; not only in its words but in its silences. A clear message of the silences in this particular text is Mr Bennet's exclusion from the arrangements which are being made. Though he has read

COMMENTARY

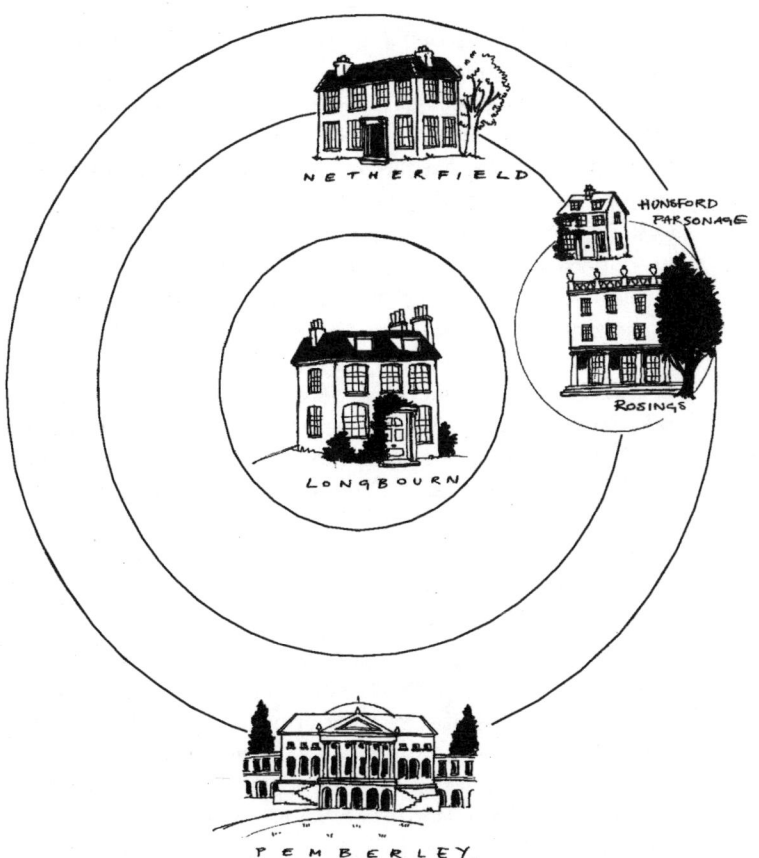

Elizabeth's expanding universe

Mr Gardiner's letter (Chapter 49, p. 317), he has to ask one of his daughters to read it, since *I hardly know myself what it is about*. It is as if he has lost all confidence in himself and his judgement. Given the shortcomings we were just discussing in his character, there is a certain fittingness that, in this moment of crisis for his family, Mr Bennet should appear to lose any paternal authority he has ever had. Darcy, Mrs Gardiner will tell Elizabeth in her letter (Chapter 52, p. 336), *did not judge your father to be a person whom he could so properly consult as your uncle* – a judgement which underlines Mr Bennet's loss of authority.

Mrs Bennet's ecstatic reaction to the letter (Chapter 49, p. 320) reminds us once more that a text can have different interpretations. Her abrupt swing from extravagant grief to wild happiness underlines the instability of a character which lacks the moral discipline to hold to any steady purpose or feeling. Her mind inactive, her life an unchanging, unchallenging round of visits, she seems to have altogether lost the capacity to think in time. With no real sense of past or future, she has no understanding that past mistakes might have consequences for future happiness. The present moment is all she can apprehend, and the news in the present moment is good: her daughter is getting married. Again, Mrs Bennet's stupidity goes beyond comedy. There is something monstrous in her infantile selfishness here (pp. 320–1), her utter indifference to the sacrifice the Gardiners appear to have made for them. There is a grotesque quality too in her preoccupation with Lydia's wedding wardrobe.

AN UNWELCOME INTERRUPTION

Chapter 52 brings Elizabeth into contact with the two men in her life. Darcy, as read about in Mrs Gardiner's letter, emerges as her family's saviour. Notice once again how Darcy comes across better when there's an intermediary – whether a companion (Bingley, Colonel Fitzwilliam) or as here a text in which his character can be read better than it can in his immediate person. Such 'texts' can of course be real pieces of writing, like this and earlier letters, but they can also be other things – his house, or his portrait, as in Chapter 43. It's a moment of great solemnity and feeling for Elizabeth, who has taken her aunt's letter to a favourite quiet spot outside, *the little copse, where she was least likely to be interrupted.* She is interrupted, though, by Wickham, who still seems to have a gift for finding his way into her secrets. His protests of affection (Chapter 52, p. 339) don't ring true; there's a bullying quality to these unsought attentions, even a hint of symbolic violation. But if there are echoes of the serpent in the Garden of Eden, Elizabeth is better prepared than Eve was. She let herself be taken in by Wickham once before, and will not do so again.

COMMENTARY

The reader cannot help wondering what is motivating Wickham here, however. Darcy sees a connection between Wickham's attempted elopement with Georgiana and his later flight with Lydia – had he not been so quick to cover up his own family's shame, he feels (Chapter 52, p. 334), he might have protected others from Wickham's attentions. The two elopements introduce a certain structural symmetry to the novel, of course, a common factor which bonds the two main characters. But might there be any deeper parallels? Darcy suggested in his letter (Chapter 35, p. 231) that while money may have been Wickham's main object in planning his elopement with Georgiana, another strong motive may have been revenge upon him. How far might revenge have been a motive in Wickham's humiliation of the Bennet family?

Clearly rattled at their last meeting (Chapter 41) by Elizabeth's scathing sarcasms, might Wickham not have carried away from Meryton a rather deeper resentment? On the face of it this may sound improbable, but if Wickham's open manner masks a deeply deceitful, calculating character, there *is* something rather obsessive in his lies. Here (Chapter 52, p. 340), for example, he is still harping on about Darcy's supposed crimes to a woman he has reason to know has long since seen through him. Publicly proven a liar, a seducer and a gambler, he is still maintaining that all he ever really wanted was to be the parson in a quiet country village!

JANE'S PAIN...

Chapter 53 brings Wickham's departure and Bingley's arrival. Jane cannot help *changing colour* (p. 342) when she hears of this. She has lost her old powers of concealment, and her feelings now speak in her face: *Lizzy could easily see that her spirits were affected ... more disturbed, more unequal, than she had often seen them* (p. 343). She still wishes she could keep her feelings to herself, however: *I can hardly bear to hear it thus perpetually talked of*, she tells Elizabeth (pp. 343–4): *My mother means well; but she does not know, no one can know how much I suffer from what she says*. This is quite an admission from the bravely bottled-up Jane, but then maybe she has needed to lose that poise which has in the past marked her down as cold and detached. (See Charlotte's remarks, Chapter 6, pp. 68–9, and Darcy's, Chapter 36, p. 237.)

And Elizabeth's

It is Elizabeth's turn to be pained by her mother when Mrs Bennet is so rude to Darcy. There's a deep **dramatic irony** here for the reader, who, like Elizabeth, knows what he has done for the family. Once again, Mrs Bennet's thoughtlessness is anything but trivial. Embarrassment, we tend to assume, is a minor affliction. Here, however, it stands for an altogether deeper humiliation. *At that instant she felt, that years of happiness could not make Jane or herself amends for moments of such painful confusion* (Chapter 53, p. 347).

Now it is Elizabeth's turn to display, despite herself, her feelings in her face: *The colour, which had been driven from her face, returned for half a minute with an additional glow, and a smile of delight added lustre to her eyes* (Chapter 53, p. 345). Jane now comes into the room, looking pale, and colours when the gentleman arrives, while Bingley looks *both pleased and embarrassed*. These few paragraphs form a little drama of their own – not spoken, though, but written in the characters' faces and gestures. Like written texts (like Mr Gardiner's letter, Chapter 49, p. 317), people may speak as eloquently in what they do not say as in what they do. *Jane was anxious that no difference should be perceived in her at all*, we find (Chapter 53, p. 348), but her silence speaks for her. Less skilled in reading Darcy's silences than her sister's, Elizabeth spends the first moments of Chapter 54 (p. 349) attempting to work out what his manner has meant.

Lady Catherine calls

After the grim farce that leads up to Bingley's proposal in Chapter 55, during which Mrs Bennet manoeuvres to remove her other daughters from the room, while Elizabeth manoeuvres to stay with her sister, there is a different sort of comic showdown in Chapter 56. Lady Catherine makes a tactical error when – like some gentleman duellist – she summons her opponent to step outside (where of course Elizabeth is in her element) rather than remaining indoors, in the humiliating context of her family. Always setting other people's houses in order, Lady Catherine conducts her own critical survey of Longbourn's interior. Outside, however, her authority ends, and Elizabeth, uncowed by Lady Catherine's haughtiness, runs rings round her in their dispute.

COMMENTARY

As she says, if the rumour of her connection with Darcy is so impossible, why does Lady Catherine ask her to deny it? Rather like Lady Catherine's musical flair (Chapter 31, p. 207), the *engagement* between Darcy and her daughter turns out to be a matter more of wishful thinking than of reality. *The engagement between them is of a peculiar kind*, she concedes. *From their infancy, they have been intended for each other.* If Darcy has *been intended* for his cousin, this does not of course mean that he has himself, in the more active form of the verb, *intended* to marry her.

Lady Catherine's threat that Elizabeth will be a social outcast if she marries Darcy (p. 365) is not just absurd but ironic. All this talk of *honour, credit, disgrace, duty* – these are terms in which it might make sense to speak of Lydia's present state, but they can have no relevance to Elizabeth's. Disgrace for Lady Catherine is a matter of social snobbery; for Jane Austen, as for Elizabeth, it is a matter of moral behaviour.

This scene has its more serious implications, then, but it is perhaps first and foremost of structural significance. As the novel draws towards its close, it gives us satisfaction, as readers, to see Elizabeth put her old oppressor down so emphatically. So the scene can be seen as balancing the episode at Rosings. More important, however, Lady Catherine's visit will prompt Darcy's second proposal (Chapter 58, p. 376). As we have seen, a character may have a function in a novel's plot which is quite different from his or her conscious motivation as a person. Again, Lady Catherine illustrates this perfectly. Her bitter enmity actually works in Elizabeth's favour.

RECOLLECTION AND RECONCILIATION

Characteristically, the understanding Elizabeth and Darcy now come to is founded on their re-reading of their own earlier encounter. They bond together in Chapter 58 by reviewing Darcy's first proposal, and the misunderstandings and mistakes it involved on both sides. They discuss the way his letter changed her view of things. Like Elizabeth and Jane, Elizabeth and Darcy can relate in their analysis of their experiences together. If thoughtlessness in *Pride and Prejudice* is a less trivial evil than we tend to consider it, thoughtfulness is a much more important force for good. It is the ability of both to learn from such analysis that has allowed them to grow as individuals, and fitted them as a couple. *You taught me a lesson, hard indeed at first, but most advantageous,* says Darcy (Chapter 58, p. 378): *By you I was properly humbled.* He has learned, the hard way, to overcome his pride, just as she has learned to overcome her prejudice. Elizabeth and Darcy have been able and willing to learn, to change, where others have not. In this respect, the experience of the characters within the action of the novel has been analogous to our own as readers. Jane Austen offers us the experience: it's up to us what we make of it. What are *you* going to make of your experience with Elizabeth, Darcy and the rest? Has your reading of *Pride and Prejudice* changed you?

Your turn

? What does Lydia's letter to Mrs Forster (Chapter 47) tell us about her character?

? Compare the reactions of Jane, Elizabeth and Mr Bennet to Mr Gardiner's letter (Chapter 49) with that of Mrs Bennet.

? *The loss of her daughter made Mrs Bennet very dull for several days,* we are told (Chapter 53, p. 341): in what sense is Lydia lost? What does Mrs Bennet mean by it, and what does Jane Austen? Make a Mini Mind Map to organise your thoughts.

? How does Jane strike Bingley now (Chapter 53)? Does Elizabeth see any difference in her sister?

well done!, you made it! But you're not through yet. Take a break now, before brainstorming

TOPICS FOR DISCUSSION AND BRAINSTORMING

One of the best ways to revise is with one or more friends. Even if you're with someone who hardly knows the text you're studying, you'll find that having to explain things to your friend will help you to organise your own thoughts and memorise key points. If you're with someone who has studied the text, you'll find that the things you can't remember are different from the things your friend can't remember – so you'll be able to help each other.

Discussion will also help you to develop interesting new ideas that perhaps neither of you would have had alone. Use a **brainstorming** approach to tackle any of the topics listed below. Allow yourself to share whatever ideas come into your head – however silly they seem. This will get you thinking creatively.

Whether alone or with a friend, use Mind Mapping (see p. vi) to help you brainstorm and organise your ideas. If with a friend, use a large sheet of paper and thick coloured pens.

Any of the topics below could feature in an exam paper, but even if you think you've found one in your actual exam, be sure to answer the precise question given.

TOPICS

1 In what ways are Elizabeth and Darcy ideally suited?
2 Mr Bennet is an irresponsible father. Discuss.
3 What part is played by *setting* in *Pride and Prejudice*?
4 With which characters do you particularly associate the title *Pride and Prejudice*? Why?
5 What do you think is the difference between 'Accomplishment' and 'Education' in *Pride and Prejudice*?
6 Mr Collins is a comic classic, but is he any more than that?
7 What part do letters play in the novel?
8 How far do social gatherings drive the action of *Pride and Prejudice*?
9 Mrs Bennet's silliness has serious consequences. Discuss.

10 What do you see as the role of class in *Pride and Prejudice*? How far are the characters defined by their social rank, and how far can they transcend it?

11 What about the role of family? How far are the characters defined by their families, and how far can they escape their background?

12 The only bad character in *Pride and Prejudice* is Wickham. Discuss.

HOW TO GET AN 'A' IN ENGLISH LITERATURE

In all your study, in coursework, and in exams, be aware of the following:

- **Characterisation** – the characters and how we know about them (e.g. what they say and do, how the author describes them), their relationships, and how they develop.
- **Plot and structure** – what happens and how it is organised into parts or episodes.
- **Setting and atmosphere** – the changing scene and how it reflects the story (e.g. the open parkland at Pemberley reflecting the liberation it offers Elizabeth).
- **Style and language** – the author's choice of words, and literary devices such as imagery, and how these reflect the mood.
- **Viewpoint** – how the story is told (e.g. through an imaginary narrator, or in the third person but through the eyes of one character – 'She was furious – how dare he!').
- **Social and historical context** – influences on the author (see 'Background' in this guide).

Develop your ability to:

- Relate **detail** to **broader content, meaning** and **style**.
- Show understanding of the author's **intentions, technique** and **meaning** (brief and appropriate comparisons with other works by the same author will gain marks).
- Give **personal response** and **interpretation**, backed up by **examples** and short **quotations**.
- **Evaluate** the author's achievement (how far does the author succeed and why?)

THE EXAM ESSAY

PLANNING

You will probably have about an hour for one essay. It is worth spending about 10 minutes planning it. An excellent way to do this is in the three stages below.

1 **Mind Map** your ideas, without worrying about their order yet.
2 **Order** the relevant ideas (the ones that really relate to the question) by numbering them in the order in which you will write the essay.
3 **Gather** your evidence and short quotes.

You could remember this as the **MOG** technique.

Now write the essay, allowing five minutes at the end for checking relevance, spelling, grammar and punctuation. **Stick to the question**, and always **back up** your points with evidence in the form of examples and short quotations. Note, you can use '...' for unimportant words missed out in a quotation.

MODEL ANSWER AND ESSAY PLAN

The next (and final) chapter consists of a model answer to an exam question on *Pride and Prejudice*, together with the Mind Map and essay plan used to write it. Don't be put off if you don't think you could write an essay to this standard yet. You'll develop your skills if you work at them. Even if you're reading this the night before your exam, you can memorise the MOG technique in order to do your personal best.

The model answer and essay plan are good examples for you to follow, but don't try to learn them off by heart. It's better to pay close attention to the wording of the question you choose to answer in the exam, and allow Mind Mapping to help you to think creatively.

Before reading the answer, you might like to do a plan of your own, then compare it with the example. The numbered points, with comments at the end, show why it's a good answer.

MODEL ANSWER AND ESSAY PLAN

QUESTION

What part does music play in *Pride and Prejudice*? Discuss in relation to three characters.

PLAN

1 Opening: culture, taste; 'accomplishment'; public performance.

2 Lady Catherine

   (a) 'accomplishment': class, culture, fashion, taste.
   (b) personal worth – 'true' enjoyment and 'natural taste'.
   (c) exposes falseness – hasn't learned.

3 Mary Bennet

   (a) motivated by 'vanity', display.
   (b) 'accomplishment' a duty.
   (c) Eliz's less 'accomplished' playing more enjoyable to listen to.
   (d) Soulless, mechanical recital shows shallow learning and morality.

4 Georgiana Darcy

   (a) Music a pleasure.
   (b) Means of communication.
   (c) Reveals emotional depths of reticent person.

5 Conclusion

True musician suggests true purpose of music – wider purpose of art for JA?

ESSAY

Music in 'Pride and Prejudice' is of particular importance for the female characters. Not only was a love of music taken to

79

PRIDE AND PREJUDICE

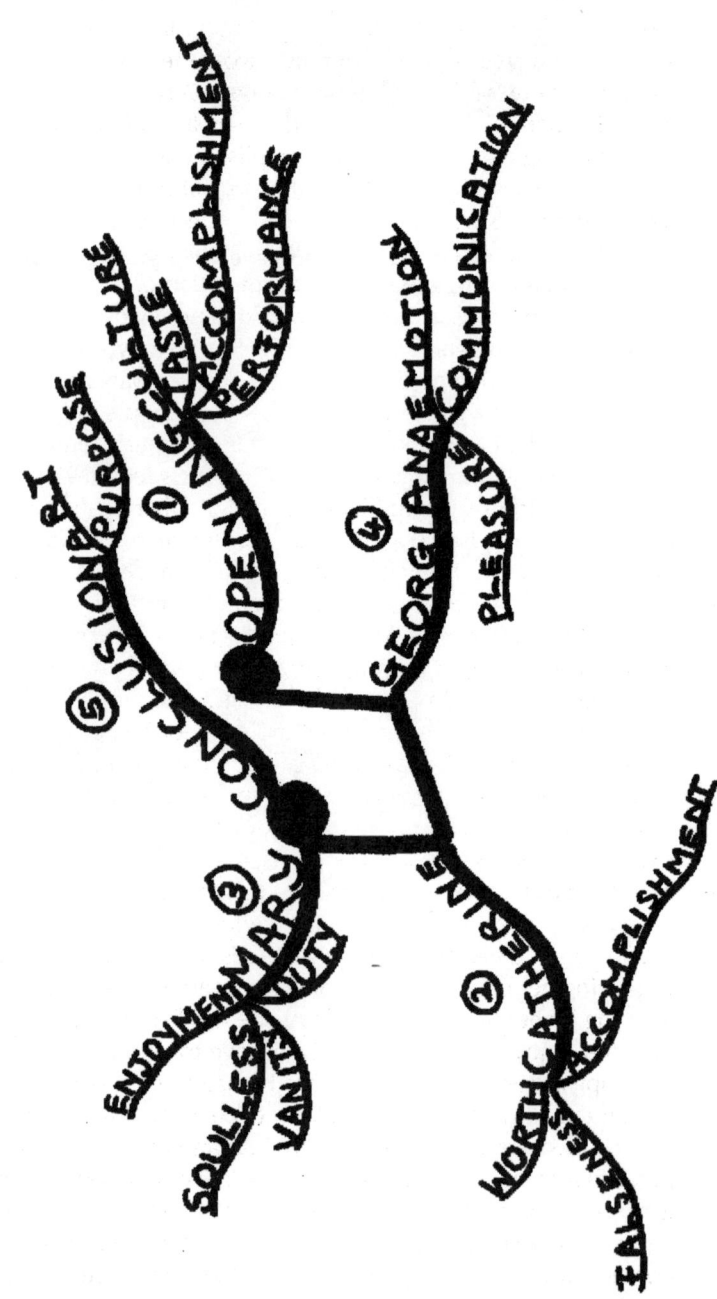

MODEL ANSWER AND ESSAY PLAN

represent a high level of culture in general in Jane Austen's society – as a taste for classical music would tend to in our own – but it was one of the 'accomplishments' every young lady needed to acquire if she was to find herself a wealthy and discriminating husband. Such 'accomplishments' included drawing, needlework and other skills too, but music was the most public (girls would play on social occasions, as Elizabeth and Mary do at the Netherfield ball in Chapter 6).[1] This makes it a natural focus for Jane Austen's examination of the idea of 'accomplishment'. Conversations would naturally develop around the piano, where sketches or embroidery would normally be considered only in quieter, more private situations.

Lady Catherine's claim that 'There are few people in England… who have more true enjoyment of music than myself' makes it clear that a liking for music is regarded as fitting in the most select individuals. Lady Catherine's snobbery would not permit her to admit to any taste which was not impeccably desirable socially. Music's importance as a mark of the individual's personal worth is apparent from Lady Catherine's insistence on her 'true enjoyment' – which is meant to set her apart from the crowd of upwardly mobile pretenders who would like it to be thought that they too have that natural taste which marks out the superior being.[2] That Lady Catherine's enthusiasm and genius for music have not, it eventually emerges, actually resulted in her attempting to learn is a delicious irony. Exposing the bogusness of her claims to musicality (and by implication, perhaps, her other pretensions), it underlines too the way in which music can become devalued as a mere mark of sophistication and class.

Like Lady Catherine, Mary Bennet sees music as a means of displaying her personal worth. She has been motivated in learning by her 'vanity', but at least she has learned! It is, however, a joyless duty for her. Girls have to gain this accomplishment, it seems, whether by nature they are musical or not; they have to work at their practice, even if they can find no pleasure in it. Their lack of pleasure comes out in their performance, however: Elizabeth's less 'accomplished' playing is more enjoyable to listen to, we are told, than Mary's 'long' (we're counting the minutes!) 'concerto'.[3] Mary's true nature comes out in her playing: her soulless, mechanical recital parallels her shallow learning and empty moralisings.

Georgiana Darcy 'does not need' Lady Catherine's advice to practise, says her brother (Chapter 31). As the housekeeper at Pemberley tells us, she 'plays and sings all day long'. This suggests that music is a pleasure for her, not a duty.[4] She plays when there's nobody there to see how 'accomplished' she is being; she plays and sings all day because, quite simply, it is what she enjoys doing. But if Georgiana has no ulterior motive in her music, it is obviously much more than an amusement for her. As deep and complex a character as either Elizabeth or Jane Bennet, but without either Elizabeth's extrovert vivacity or the physical beauty that proclaims Jane's inner beauty to the world, Georgiana can find in music a way of articulating feelings she could not otherwise gain access to. If music exposes Mary Bennet's shallowness, it reveals Georgiana's emotional depth.[5]

In this true musician, perhaps, we find Jane Austen's own vision of what music really ought to be: not just an empty accomplishment but a means of gaining and giving pleasure – and at the same time of exploring, and communicating, the deepest emotions of human existence. In this way, Georgiana's music can be seen as standing for Jane Austen's writing. If Jane Austen's own pleasure in writing is obvious from our own pleasure in reading her, she could also articulate in novels like 'Pride and Prejudice' a profound and original view of human life.[6]

WHAT'S SO GOOD ABOUT IT?

1 Shows an awareness of the novel's historical and social background.
2 Good use of quotation, considering not only the main point of what the speaker says but its more detailed emphasis and implications.
3 Shows appreciation of the subtler points of Jane Austen's humour.
4 Examples from the text are used here to back up an assertion.
5 Giving each character under discussion a paragraph of her own, this middle section of the essay shows an awareness of how apparently minor characters can help present a novel's central themes.
6 As the essay approaches its conclusion, it moves out from the detail of its individual character analyses to consider their implications for Jane Austen's work as a whole.

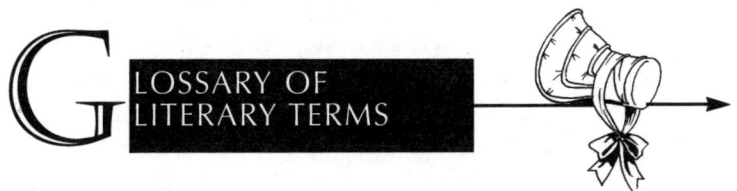

Glossary of Literary Terms

alliteration repetition of a sound at the beginnings of words; e.g. *ladies' lips.*

context the social and historical influences on the author.

foreshadowing an indirect warning of things to come, often through imagery.

image a word picture used to make an idea come alive; e.g. a metaphor, simile, or personification (see separate entries).

imagery the kind of word picture used to make an idea come alive.

irony (1) where the author or a character says the opposite of what they really think, or pretends ignorance of the true facts, usually for the sake of humour or ridicule; (2) where events turn out in what seems a particularly inappropriate way, as if mocking human effort.

metaphor a description of a thing as if it were something essentially different but also in some way similar; e.g. *we must stem the tide of malice* (Mary, Ch. 47).

personification a description of something (e.g. fate) as if it were a person.

prose language in which, unlike verse, there is no set number of syllables in a line, and no rhyming.

rhetorical question one asked for effect or as a figure of speech, expecting no answer; e.g. *Do you think it incredible that Mr Collins should be able to procure any woman's good opinion, because he was not so happy as to succeed with you?* (Charlotte, Ch. 22).

setting the place in which the action occurs, usually affecting the atmosphere; e.g. the spacious grounds of Pemberley.

simile   a comparison of two things which are different in most ways but similar in one important way; e.g. *Her voice rang like a bell.*

structure   how the plot is organised.

theme   an idea explored by an author; e.g. gentility.

viewpoint   how the story is told; e.g. in direct narrative in the author's own 'voice', in discussion between characters, or in a letter from one character to another.

Index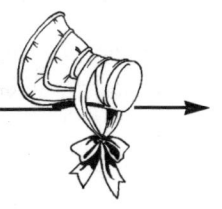

accomplishments 3, 23–4, 47, 58, 80–2

Bennet, Elizabeth 12, 31–2, 35–6, 45–6, 48, 49–52, 59, 64, 72, 73–4
Bennet, Jane 13, 33, 53–4, 55, 58, 71
Bennet, Kitty 15
Bennet, Lydia 15, 57, 58, 67–8
Bennet, Mary 15, 25, 58, 80, 81
Bennet, Mr 14, 30, 59, 67, 68–9
Bennet, Mrs 14, 30, 67, 70
Bingley, Caroline (Miss) 36, 65
Bingley, Mr 16, 31, 63
brainstorming ix, 75

Collins, Mr 17–18, 38, 40–1

Darcy, Georgiana 23, 54, 63, 65, 80, 81–2
Darcy, Mr 13, 31–2, 49–56, 62, 63–4, 66, 70, 73–4
De Bourgh, Lady Catherine 18, 46–7, 49, 72–3, 80, 81

family 20–1, 30, 35, 36, 40, 55–6, 57, 60, 63, 65, 66, 69

Gardiner, Mrs 17, 43, 63–4
gentility 2, 22–3, 32, 46, 48, 65
growth 26–8, 31, 37, 38, 43, 45–6, 47, 48, 51, 53, 56, 58, 59, 62, 68, 74

Lucas, Charlotte 17, 33–4, 42–3, 50

marriage 3–4, 21–2, 30, 32, 33, 42–3, 59
MOG technique 78

Pemberley 61–2, 64–5

reading 24–6, 30, 32, 33, 40, 41, 44, 50, 53, 54–6, 59, 60, 61–2, 63–4, 66, 67–9

style and language 46, 48, 49, 54–5, 57, 61–2, 63, 64, 65, 73

themes 20–7

Wickham, Mr 16, 38–9, 44–5, 54, 55, 59, 70–1

BUZAN TRAINING COURSES

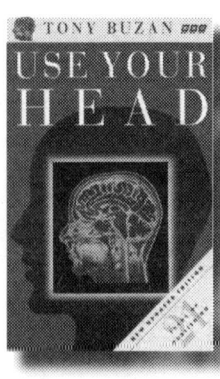

For further information on books, video and audio tapes, support materials and courses, please send for our brochure.

Buzan Centres Ltd, 54 Parkstone Road, Poole, Dorset, BH15 2PX
Tel: 44 (0) 1202 674676, Fax: 44 (0) 1202 674776
Email: Buzan_Centres_Ltd@compuserve.com